GOTHA AIRCRAFT

GOTHA
AIRCRAFT
1913–1954
FROM **THE LONDON BOMBER** TO **THE FLYING WING JET FIGHTER**

ANDREAS METZMACHER

www.fonthillmedia.com
office@fonthillmedia.com

First published in the United Kingdom
and the United States of America 2021

British Library Cataloguing in Publication Data:
A catalogue record for this book is available from the British Library

Copyright © Andreas Metzmacher 2021

ISBN 978-1-78155-706-8

The right of Andreas Metzmacher to be identified as the author of
this work has been asserted by him in accordance with the Copyright,
Designs and Patents Act 1988.

All rights reserved. No part of this publication may be reproduced,
stored in a retrieval system or transmitted in any form or by any means,
electronic, mechanical, photocopying, recording or otherwise, without
prior permission in writing from Fonthill Media Limited

Typeset in 10.5pt on 13.5pt Sabon
Printed and bound in England

Contents

1	1883–1913: From the Carousel to Cargo Trains: The Beginning of the Gotha Wagon Factory	7
2	1913–1918: 3 February 1913: The Founding of Division II Aircraft Works	11
3	Aircraft 1913–1918	15
4	VGO—Giant Aircraft from Gotha-East	49
5	Gotha Seaplanes	52
6	1919–1933: Suspension of Aircraft Construction	79
7	1933–1945: Gotha Wagon Factory Produces Aircraft Again	83
8	Aircraft 1933–1945	93
9	Aircraft Produced Under Licence	113
10	Projects 1935–1945	129
11	1945–1953: Allied Occupation, Dismantling and Reconstruction	140
12	1953–1954: Gliders for the GDR	143
13	1954–2017: Socialist Planned Economy and Reprivatisation	149
	Epilogue and Acknowledgements	151
	Appendix	152
	Abbreviations	156
	Bibliography	157
	Endnotes	158

1

1883–1913:
From the Carousel to Cargo Trains:
The Beginning of the Gotha Wagon Factory

The main business of the Gotha wagon factory was, as the name suggests, the construction of railway carriages and wagons, but it was through the construction of aircraft that the company would later become internationally known. The roots of the company, however, come from a completely different origin. Everything started on 2 October 1883, for on this day, the locksmith Fritz Bothmann founded a small carousel factory in Gotha, which was at that time the residence and capital of the small German Duchy of Saxony-Coburg and Gotha. In 1889, businessman Louis Glück became involved with the company and the name was changed to Bothmann & Glück. This change was accompanied by the gradual increase in the production profile. In addition to swings and transportation vans for showmen, in 1894 Bothmann & Glück also began building railway vehicles such as freight cars and trams. On 30 July 1898, the company transformed into a joint stock corporation with fresh capital and was now entered in the commercial register[1] as Gothaer Waggonfabrik, formerly Fritz Bothmann & Glück Aktiengesellschaft. After the two founders left the company—Louis Glück in 1900 and Fritz Bothmann two years later—it was renamed to Gothaer Waggonfabrik AG (GWF). Albert Kandt (1866–1926) moved up to the boardroom and soon became the general manager. Thanks to him and Duke Carl Eduard of Saxony-Coburg and Gotha (1884–1954), who ruled Gotha at the time, GWF also entered aircraft construction shortly thereafter. The duke and grandson of Queen Victoria, born in Claremont House in England, was a great patron of aviation in his small duchy of Thuringia. Because of his involvement with the Zeppelin Society and Deutsche Luftschifffahrts AG, an airship hangar was built by the Düsseldorf-based company Stephansdach in Gotha in 1909. 'Aviation will play an important role in the lives of people everywhere in the not too distant future.' With these words, Duke Carl Eduard inaugurated the Carl Eduard airship hangar on 9 July 1910—and thus gave the go-ahead for an eventful Gotha aviation history. From then on, things progressed very quickly.

Almost two years later, an aviation school, the Carl Eduard Aviation School, was founded next to the airship hangar. *Aviatik*, an aircraft manufacturer from Alsace, provided personnel and technology, two flight instructors, two mechanics, a monoplane, and a biplane. One of the flight instructors was Ernst Schlegel (1882–1978), later the first chief pilot of the Gothaer Waggonfabrik. At that time, a fundraising campaign in the German Reich prompted German industry to make targeted investments in aircraft construction. On 21 April 1912, at the suggestion of the flight pioneer August Euler, Prince Heinrich of Prussia called for a 'national flight donation'. The aim of this fundraiser was to promote aviation in the German Empire and to reduce the developmental gap in comparison to other nations, but most importantly with arch-rival France. The funds donated were to primarily be used to finance flight competitions, award prizes, and train civil pilots. The plan worked and the incentive was created for German industry to build and further develop aircraft and aircraft engines in series. It was planned that the aircraft would primarily be purchased by the military. The plan worked. The national flight donation was a huge success. The Germans donated the, at the time, enormous sum of 7.6 million German marks by 1913. Thanks to the prizes awarded, aviation in Germany experienced an unprecedented surge up to the beginning of the First World War. The era of aviation pioneers came to a conclusive end through this development. Distribution of awards from the national flight donation was subject to specific conditions. One of the stipulations was that the aircraft construction companies needed to maintain their own flight schools, which had to be equipped with self-built aircraft. Due to these regulations, flight schools with no connection to aviation manufacturers were excluded from the award system from the outset. The selection of future civilian flight students lay with the flight schools, which also bore the risk of training. Only after passing the flight test was the aviation school able to claim a reward of 8,000 marks from the national flight donation funds. The training was thus free of charge for the flight students; however, they had to commit to being available to the air force in the event of war. In various national flight competitions such as the Prince Heinrich flight, high premiums were also distributed to the winners and the aircraft manufacturers. It promised to be a worthwhile business. With the economic infrastructure in place, it was the right time for Gothaer Waggonfabrik to start making aircraft. The groundbreaking ceremony for two new production halls for future aircraft construction on the factory premises in Gotha-Ost took place at the end of 1912. In the same year, the Gotha section of the 'Reichsfliegerverein' (Imperial Flying Association) was founded. Its first chairman was none other than Albert Kandt, the director of the Gothaer Waggonfabrik. Together with the imperial Aero Club and under the patronage of Duke Carl Eduard of Saxony-Coburg and Gotha, the Gotha Aviation Association immediately organised their first aeroplane competition. The event, without the participation of Gotha aircraft and pilots, took place from 17–19 August 1912 at the Boxberg horseracing track near Gotha. In addition to a speed and altitude competition, a key part of the competition was the proficiency of targeted bombing runs.

The Willing Monoplane: The First Aircraft from Gotha

Even before the new production halls in Gotha-Ost were completed, Kandt supported the construction of a monoplane by the designer Karl Willing (1885–1956), who came from Neudietendorf, near Gotha. Willing had already built two planes, but when his last monoplane broke, his financial options were exhausted. Willing turned to Kandt, who eagerly offered him financial and material support for the construction of a new aircraft, leaving the GWF workshop on Langensalzaer Strasse for him. Kandt presented the still-uncovered monoplane, which was equipped with a four-cylinder in-line engine and 50 hp, to the military in August 1912. The officers had travelled to the Aeroplan tournament on the Gotha Boxberg. However, the innovative design of the tubular steel fuselage and the wooden wings was too daring for them, so they rejected Willing's design. The plane was scrapped without ever being built and given the chance to try flying. It was not particularly farsighted. A few years later, Willing's technology, the so-called mixed construction, became the cutting edge technology of the time and a design feature of almost all Gotha aircraft.

Karl Willing (left) in the summer of 1912 in front of his monoplane in Gotha. After the failure of his last aircraft project, Willing worked as a technical assistant at GWF until the war began before he was drafted into the forces. (*Krieg collection*)

2

1913–1918:

3 FEBRUARY 1913:

The Founding of Division II Aircraft Works

After all the preparatory work had been completed, Albert Kandt founded the 'Division II Aircraft Works' of the Gothaer Waggonfabrik on 3 February 1913. At the same time, he took over the Carl Eduard Aviation School, which, with its director Ernst Schlegel, moved from the airship port in the south of the city next to the wagon factory. From 1 April 1913, Kandt hired well-known flight pioneer and engineer Karl Grulich (1881–1949) as technical manager of the new department. Designers Schmieder, Bartl, and Böhnisch came to Gotha from the Etrich pilot plants in Libau, Silesia. They brought along the licence-free construction documents of the Etrich-Taube. It was then rebuilt and further developed in Gotha. Finally, Director-General Kandt offered former cyclist and racing driver Bruno Büchner (1871–1943), who was currently enthusiastic about aviation, the opportunity to implement his plans for the construction of aircraft in Gotha. At that time, Büchner was also successful in many German flight competitions. He came to Gotha as a flight instructor at the beginning of 1913 through the Aviatik company, which also provided the training aircraft of the Carl Eduard Aviation School. Büchner's guest appearance here was quite short. The GWF built planes according to Büchner's plans, however, that was all that went according to his plans. Officially, these were not considered GWF constructions. Büchner's first aircraft was a single-engined biplane with a 70-hp Argus engine, but it is not known whether this aircraft ever flew. Büchner's second design was a single-engined biplane with a lattice fuselage, two floats, and a 100-hp Mercedes engine with a pusher propeller. Büchner wanted to take part in a water flight competition on Lake Constance in the summer of 1913. Due to illness, he had to cancel his participation and this ended Bruno Büchner's stay in Gotha.

On 1 October 1914, Director-General Kandt was able to bring a talented designer to Gotha with the Swiss Hans Burkhard (1888–1977). Burkhard started his career at Rumpler in Berlin and had most recently been employed by the

The Büchner biplane from 1913. If you look closely, you can see a retouched person standing next to the plane on this original press photo of Gothaer Waggonfabrik. It may be Bruno Büchner. In the background you can see Schloss Friedenstein, residence of Duke Carl Eduard. (*Krieg collection*)

Aerial view of Gothaer Waggonfabrik around 1915: In addition to several biplanes, some Gotha-Tauben (Gotha-Doves) can be seen on the factory airfield. At the front of the picture is the airfield of the Pilot Training Department 3 (FEA 3). The two adjacent airfields initially attracted so many onlookers from the residents of Gotha, that Director-General Kandt asked the city of Gotha to deploy police officers to safeguard flight operations. Nevertheless, incidents occurred repeatedly. A constant problem was caused by farmers, who continuously cut across the airfield as a shortcut on their way to their fields. This often led to hair-raising situations and accidents. (*DEHLA*)

Deutsche Bristol-Werken (German Bristol works) in Halberstadt. After arriving in Gotha, Burkhard took over the construction of land planes at GWF, which designer Karl Rösner, who had been hired on 1 September 1913 to handle the seaplane construction, had temporarily taken over. On 16 March 1915, the Gotha wagon factory had to deal with a departure. Technical manager Karl Grulich, who was only hired in 1913, left Gotha, evidently after differences with Kandt. Of all the places he could have gone, Grulich changed to the head of the design office of the direct competitor to GWF, the Flugzeugbau Friedrichshafen (FF).

Karl Grulich, Aircraft Designer

The mechanical engineer, born in Halle an der Saale in 1881, became a designer and chief engineer at Harlan Werke GmbH in Berlin-Johannisthal in 1910. After an unintentional test flight with a Harlan monoplane he had designed, he taught himself how to fly. Officially, he acquired German FAI Patent no. 46, issued by the German Airship Association, on 29 December 1910. On 22 January 1912, he took off from Johannisthal with three passengers on board and set a world flight-time record of two hours, two minutes, and forty-five seconds.

After the bankruptcy of Harlan Werke in March 1913, Albert Kandt hired him on 1 April 1913 as technical director of the newly founded aircraft construction department of the GWF. Two years later, he switched to the office of aircraft construction at Friedrichshafen on Lake Constance, a direct competitor of the Gothaer Waggonfabrik in the manufacture of large aircraft for the air force and single-engined reconnaissance aircraft for the navy. The company belonged proportionally to Count Ferdinand von Zeppelin. At the end of the war, GWF was no longer able to mass-produce its own designs in sufficient numbers; because of this, aircraft from other manufacturers were to be built under licence. These turned out to be designs from Flugzeugbau Friedrichshafen. After the war, the aviation pioneer joined the still-young business of commercial aviation. In 1926, he became technical director of Deutsche Luft Hansa. Fokker commercial aircraft modified by Grulich were part of the newly established airline's first stock. Karl Grulich died in 1949.

From 1913 to 1915, the flight pioneer and engineer Karl Grulich was technical director of the aircraft construction department. (*DEHLA*)

3

Aircraft 1913–1918

Gotha LE 1—Training Aircraft

Before the first completely independent constructions were created in Gotha, the new department gained experience in the reconstruction of tried and tested aircraft models, which were gradually improved. The first Gotha aircraft built in series was a copy of the well-known Etrich-Rumpler Taube, which was called Gotha LE 1 (LE—*Landeindecker*, land monoplane). On 23 April 1913, the first replica took off for its maiden flight in Gotha. A total of ten Gotha LE 1s were built. The flight school of the German aviation pioneer Karl Caspar received six planes in Hamburg, the other four remained in Gotha and were used by the Carl Eduard flight school. On a Gotha LE 1, from 10 to 17 May 1913, Lieutenant August Joly took part in a national reliability competition, the Prince Heinrich flight. After everything was said and done, Joly was able to finish fourth overall. It was the first flight competition in which an aircraft that had been produced in Gotha took part.

Gotha LE 2—The 'Gotha Taube', Training Aircraft and Reconnaissance Aircraft

Parallel to the ongoing production of the LE 1, engineers Böhnisch and Bartl further developed the basic construction of the Etrich Taube as the Gotha LE 2. They reinforced the fuselage and the wings, replaced the Blériot undercarriage with a stronger V-undercarriage, and mounted a rounded rudder. A six-cylinder in-line engine from Mercedes with 100 hp was used as the engine. Instead of the Mercedes engine, some LE 2s in the series production also received Oberursel rotary engines or Rapp in-line engines.

GWF chief pilot Ernst Schlegel (*front*) in a Gotha LE 1. The monoplane is a replica of the Etrich-Taube. (*Gotha city archive, signature 6.1/1417 image 6*)

Continuing into 1913, some of these machines participated very successfully in various German flight competitions. Karl Caspar took third place during the East Prussian round-trip flight competition on 9–13 August 1913 for civil aviators. On 16 October 1913, Caspar took part in a long-distance competition hosted by the national flight donation and achieved third place by flying 1,381 kilometres. The prize: 50,000 marks. A Gotha-Taube placed directly in front of him: GWF chief pilot Ernst Schlegel earned second place; he reached 1,497 kilometres and won 60,000 marks. The military was also impressed by the good flight characteristics and the high manufacturing quality of the Gotha LE 2. The Prussian army administration ordered a total of 20 military 'Tauben', which were used as training and reconnaissance aircraft.

GWF delivered 14 aircraft to the Döberitz pilot school near Berlin, the other six to the military pilot station in Cologne. After the outbreak of war, most of the 'Taube' were used on the front as reconnaissance aircraft. On 26 October 1914, a Gotha Taube LE 2 of the Field Aviation Department (FFA) 9 wrote aviation history when it became the first German military aircraft to fly over the English Channel and drop two bombs over the English port city of Dover. The pilot of the plane was none other than Karl Caspar, who had since moved into the reserve as a lieutenant. For five and a half hours, he was said to have been in the air with his observer, Lieutenant Werner Roos—which was also record-breaking at the time.

Production of Gotha LE 2 in GWF around 1913–14. (*Author's collection*)

The improved Gotha LE 2 emerged from the Gotha LE 1. After the outbreak of war, this type was used as a reconnaissance aircraft on some sections of the front. (*DEHLA*)

A presumably recreated photo showing Karl Caspar and Werner Roos in their Gotha LE 2 after the first bomb attack on Dover on 26 October 1914. (*Stiftung Deutsches Technikmuseum Berlin*)

Karl Caspar, Aviation Pioneer

Karl Caspar (1883–1954), the holder of German FAI Patent no. 77, dated 27 March 1911, filed on Rumpler Taube, was a well-known German aviation pioneer. In the pre-war period, he participated very successfully in various flight competitions. For example, he was able to set several distance and altitude records on the Gotha Taube. Caspar owned his own flight school in Hamburg, later even his own aircraft factory, the Hanseatische Flugzeugwerke Karl Caspar AG. Shortly after Caspar was drafted into the Imperial German Flying Corps on 2 August 1914 as a lieutenant in the reserve, the company merged with Brandenburgische Flugzeugwerke GmbH to form Hansa- und Brandenburgische Flugzeugwerke AG, whose chief designer was Ernst Heinkel. His attack in a Gotha LE 2 on Dover on 26 October 1914 was a daring piece of work. In 1916, Caspar left the military service and was bought out of his share of the Hansa and Brandenburg aircraft factories. Starting in July 1917, Caspar's company took over the repair of Gotha aircraft. The Hanseatische Flugzeugwerke Karl Caspar AG existed until 1928 when it went bankrupt due to a lack of orders. The Reichsmarine (German Navy 1919–1935) took over the remnants of the insolvent company and set up a camouflaged testing facility here.

Karl Caspar in front of a Gotha LE 1. Caspar's flight school in Hamburg was the purchaser of the first Gotha Taube built in series. (*DEHLA*)

Gotha LE 3—Training Aircraft, Reconnaissance Aircraft

The Gotha LE 3 is an LE 2 that was further improved at the beginning of 1914 by Grulich and Bartl. In addition, the chassis was revised again and the tensioning of the wings simplified. In several production lots, a total of 57 machines are said to have been ordered for the Imperial German Flying Corps, 54 of which had been delivered and three cancelled by the beginning of 1915. At the beginning of the war, Gotha LE 3s were seen as scouts over some front sections. However, the slow and maintenance-prone aircraft was not only technically obsolete, but also its flying capabilities were outdated and it disappeared relatively quickly from the armed forces' arsenal. The last built LE 3, which was delivered on 7 July 1915, therefore never arrived at the front, but was immediately handed over to the FEA 3 in Gotha. FEA 3 was located in Darmstadt until 18 February 1915 and then moved to Gotha. The Carl Eduard Aviation School was thus superfluous and was replaced by the military operation of the FEA 3. The department then became the preferred buyer of the GWF's school and reconnaissance aircraft, which were often only built in small series and which were not, or no longer, considered fit for the front.

The Gotha LE 3 was the last Taube design from GWF that was produced in series. A total 54 machines were built. (*Stiftung Deutsches Technikmuseum Berlin*)

Gotha LE 4—Training Aircraft

The end and highlight of the 'Taube development' at GWF was the Gotha LE 4, a unique piece that Gotha engineer Karl Rösner had previously developed in early 1914 specifically for the Prince Heinrich flight. The Prince Heinrich flight, which came about under the patronage of Prince Heinrich of Prussia, took place on 17 May 1914. Only German aircraft designs that met the requirements of an army aircraft were permitted. For this purpose, Rösner completely redesigned the LE 4 aircraft, which, apart from the classic dove shape of the wings, differed significantly from its predecessors. The control surfaces consisted of a tubular steel frame and the elevator could be folded up for transport on the fuselage. The fully clad Mercedes D I in-line engine with 100 hp had a modern head cooler instead of the side cooler previously attached to the fuselage. The aircraft made a modern impression, but still had a crucial weak point. Rösner had given the relatively heavy machine a landing gear that was much too light. During the first stage of the competition from Darmstadt to Frankfurt am Main, the plane broke when it landed after Schlegel had touched a fence with the propeller and landing gear. The damage to the aircraft could not be repaired on site, so GWF chief pilot Ernst Schlegel retired from the competition. The plane was 'not worth much' Schlegel later said. The Carl Eduard Aviation School received the LE 4 after it had been rebuilt.

The Gotha LE 4 was a one-off. The aircraft was specially developed for the Prince Heinrich flight. (*Author's collection*)

Gotha LD 1—Reconnaissance and Training Aircraft

At the beginning of 1914, the era of biplanes commence at Gotha with two models: the LD 2 and the LD 1 (LD—*Landdoppeldecker*, land biplane), which were designed by Karl Rösner. GWF received the order to build the LD 1 on 31 March 1914, almost a month after the LD 2. The LD 1, later also referred to as the B I type, was a two-strut biplane whose wings were slightly arrow shaped. Rösner used the tail unit from the Gotha LE 4, the last Gotha-Taube. The plane is said to have been 210 kg lighter than the LD 2. Various engines were tested on the aircraft. Ultimately, the decision was made to use the nine-cylinder Oberursel U 1 100-hp rotary engine, a further development of the French Gnome engine, which was built under licence in Oberursel. As with the LE 4, the drive disappeared behind a closed hood.

In this form, the prototype took part in the 1914 East Prussia round-trip flight. It turned out that the engine, when located behind the closed hood, did not get enough cooling; as a result, the lower part of the hood was cut off on site and the rotating cylinders of the motor were exposed. In this modified form, the aircraft was designated LD 1a. On 24 August 1914, GWF was commissioned by Idflieg to produce a small series of ten planes. However, because the Oberursel rotary engines were initially made available primarily for combat fighters from the manufacturers Fokker and Pfalz, the aircraft were delivered a good one and a half years later on 12 April 1916. When the ten LD 1as were finally finished, the construction had long been overtaken by technical progress and the aircraft were hopelessly out of date. All ten LD 1as therefore stayed in Gotha, where the FEA 3 used them for training purposes.

Gotha LD 2—Reconnaissance Aircraft

On 24 February 1914, the Prussian army administration commissioned GWF to build the Gotha LD 2, a two-seater biplane for reconnaissance with an engine that produced 100 hp, a wingspan of up to 12 metres, and a top speed of 90 kph. The three-handled biplane designed by Rösner was then equipped with a 100-hp Mercedes D I, with side coolers on the fuselage and a three-legged [tricycle?] landing gear. The prototype of the LD 2 was taken on 31 August 1914 by the Field Pilot Division 4 and flew with the military number B. 458/14 as an unarmed reconnaissance aircraft on the Western Front. On 24 August 1914, the inspectorate of the Imperial German Flying Corps (Idflieg) ordered nine more LD 2s from Gotha. The aircraft, also known as Gotha B.II, were delivered to the FEA 3 in Gotha on 12 April 1915. Six LD 2s were later handed over to the Ottoman Empire as training aircraft.

Gotha LD 3 and LD 4—Training Aircraft

While the LD 1 and the LD 2 were constructions of their own, the Gotha aircraft manufacturers built the French Caudron G III under licence as Gotha LD 3 at the end of 1913. The two-seater biplane was equipped like the original with an air-cooled 50-hp Gnome rotary engine. The pilot and observer sat one behind the other. During a test flight of the prototype by GWF chief pilot Ernst Schlegel, the propeller and parts of the engine cowling flew off the aircraft at an altitude of 2,000 metres. Schlegel managed to bring the now non-powered aircraft back to the ground safely thanks to the good gliding properties. This was one of the positive characteristics that made the LD 3 particularly suitable as an ideal connecting aircraft. Nevertheless, the machine remained a one-off. On 26 March 1914, GWF was commissioned to construct a modified version of the LD 3 with a more powerful 100-hp Gnome engine and a wider fuselage in which the pilot and observer were to sit side by side. All other dimensions, such as the wingspan and length, were identical to the LD 3 except for the increased mass. However, like the LD 3, the Prussian Army Administration also rejected the construction of the LD 4. Both aircraft then ended up in the hands of the Carl Eduard Aviation School.

The Gotha LD 1 was the first biplane of GWF. The aircraft was designed by Karl Rösner. (*DEHLA*)

The somewhat larger Gotha LD 2 was designed by Rösner parallel to the LD 1. Ten of these aircraft were built, which, apart from the prototypes, were not used at the front. (*DEHLA*)

GWF chief pilot Ernst Schlegel in front of the Gotha LD 3: The construction of the aircraft was considered to be too light with its wire-braced bamboo struts, the licence-built machine by the French Caudron G III, did not prevail. (*DEHLA*)

The Gotha LD 4 had an engine that was twice as powerful as the LD 3 and the pilot and observer sat side by side. The photograph was taken during the secondary programme of the Prince Heinrich flight in Hamburg in 1914. The LD 4, in which only German constructions with a German engine were allowed to participate, did not take part in the competition. (*DEHLA*)

Ernst Schlegel, Chief Pilot of the Gotha Wagon Factory

The son of a locomotive driver, born in Constance on Lake Constance in 1882, Schlegel was a real flight pioneer, an 'old eagle'—this was the name given to the German pilots who had earned their pilot's licence before the First World War. Schlegel was enthusiastic about aviation early on and, together with a friend, built their first aircraft in 1910, which was completely destroyed during a flight attempt. In 1911, he was hired as an auxiliary designer at the Aviatik company in Mulhouse, Alsace, where he was involved in the construction of a monoplane. It was in this monoplane that Schlegel learned how to fly. On 10 April 1912, he successfully passed his flight test, and his German FAI patent bears the number 209. Shortly afterwards, he became head and flight instructor of the Carl Eduard Aviation School in Gotha, and after the founding of the aircraft construction department at GWF, he became its first head pilot. Schlegel also became known throughout Germany for his success in national flight competitions, especially for cross-country flights. He took third place in his Aviatik monoplane at the Prince Heinrich flight in 1913—ahead of the military pilot Lieutenant Joly, who took part in the competition with one of the first Gotha LE 1s. As early as 10 January 1914, Schlegel was able to record his 2,000th flight in his logbook. At the beginning of August 1914, he was supposed to represent the Gotha wagon factory at the seaplane competition in Warnemünde, when the war broke out. Schlegel never returned to Gotha. He volunteered for military service at the Flieger-Ersatz-Abteilung (FEA) 5 (the department responsible for training new pilots for the front) in Hanover and immediately landed on the Western Front. At the end of 1914, he became a parking engineer at an army air park, where he had the task of taking off the aircraft that were delivered for the front. In 1917, he was assigned to Idflieg for construction supervision at the Rumpler company, and the following year, Schlegel was hired as a civil chief engineer and head of aviation at the Pfalz-Flugzeugwerke in Speyer. After the war, he built up a regional network for passenger flights from Constance Airfield with six former military aircraft. From 1923 to 1935, Schlegel lived in Switzerland, and after his return to Germany, he was employed as a senior engineer at the *Reichsluftfahrtministerium* (Reich Aviation Ministry—RLM) until 1944. The 'old eagle' died in 1978 in his hometown of Constance at the age of 94.

Gotha LD 5— Cavalry Aircraft

The Gotha LD 5 was the first draft developed by the Swiss designer Hans Burkhard for the Gotha wagon factory. The aircraft was built in 1914 on request of Idflieg, who required a light biplane to explore the terrain for the cavalry units—the reason why the model was identified as a cavalry plane. The small twin-bay biplane had a span of 8.5 metres and was equipped with a Oberursel rotary engine with 100 hp and integral propeller. On 12 December 1914, the first

GWF chief pilot Ernst Schlegel in front of a Gotha LE 3. (*DEHLA*)

The biplane Gotha LD 5 was the first construction of Swiss-born Hans Burkhard for GWF. (*DEHLA*)

LD 5 was completed. Unfortunately, no one wanted this design anymore; a special aircraft for the cavalry was no longer required in the stagnant, positional war. Due to these developments, the innovative equipment was no longer produced. The LD 5 was to be equipped with a synchronized machine gun that fired through the propeller circle, thus the aircraft could have been used as a light combat vehicle. Altogether, a total of 13 unarmed LD 5s are said to have been built in three construction lots, all of which did not reach the front, but were instead handed over to the FEA 3 in Gotha.

Gotha LD 6—Reconnaissance Aircraft

In December 1914, Idflieg commissioned GWF with the design of a single-engined biplane for the remote reconnaissance, which should also be able to drop bombs. Karl Rösner then constructed a two-bay biplane with a 150-hp Benz Bz.III engine. The aircraft was considered a further development of the Gotha LD 2. Among other things, the surfaces on the elevator and rudder were completely new. The machine had its first flight on 17 December 1914, and with new GWF chief pilot Oswald Kahnt at the controls, the prototype crashed on 30 January 1915 in gusty weather from a high altitude; the aircraft went up in flames, and Kahnt was killed instantly. As a replacement, GWF built a modified model, which was referred to as Gotha LD 6a. GWF could have saved themselves the effort. The Prussian army administration refused a series production of the aircraft. The FEA 3 received the one and only aircraft that had been produced to be used as a trainer aircraft.

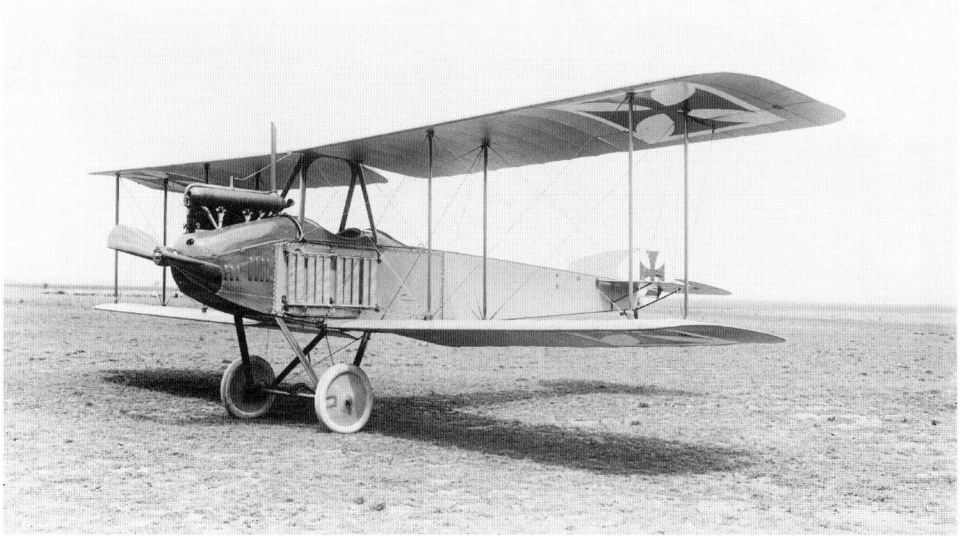

On 30 January 1915, GWF chief pilot Oswald Kahnt crashed with the prototype of the LD 6 and was killed. The picture shows the newly built Gotha LD 6a. (*Stadtarchiv Gotha, signature 6.1/1417 picture 12*)

Gotha LD 7—Reconnaissance and Training Aircraft

The Gotha LD 7 was the last single-engined biplane of the LD development series. The aircraft was released on 19 May 1915 by Idflieg as a reconnaissance aircraft. The designer was Hans Burkhard. The twin-bay biplane was equipped with a 120-hp Mercedes D II engine and side radiators attached to the rear fuselage. A small series of at least 18 aircraft left the Gotha factory hangars at the end of August 1915—a somewhat reconciliatory conclusion of the otherwise less successful LD series. However, even the LD 7 was considered outdated at delivery and prevailed just as little as the other LD models of GWF that came before when compared to the competition models of other German manufacturers. The plane never made it to the front and was used exclusively for training purposes. Five LD 7s remained with the FEA 3 in Gotha, and five more were received by the Imperial German Flying Corps in Turkey.

Gotha G I—Armed Escort Aircraft, Bomber

The Gotha G I is considered, along with the simultaneously developed AEG KI, to be the first twin-engined fighter aircraft of the Imperial German Flying Corps. The construction was based on a design by Oskar Ursinus (1878–1952). The engineer and publisher of the German aeronautical magazine *Flugsport* completed his military service in the FEA 3, which was still based in Darmstadt at the beginning of August 1914. The leader of the FEA 3 was Major Georg Friedel. Ursinus presented the draft of a twin-engined escort aircraft, which was to protect

The LD 7 very similar to the Gotha LD 6 which formed the conclusion of the less successful LD series. (*DEHLA*)

the, at that time still unarmed, reconnaissance aircraft over the front. Friedel was not only convinced by the project, but also provided Ursinus with material and craftsmen for the construction of a prototype. The twin-engined innovative design of the biplane was new to German aircraft construction at the time. The fuselage was attached to the upper wing of the biplane and the engines were mounted close to each other on the lower wing. This was done to ensure a safe and stable flight even in the event of an engine failure. Ursinus patented this construction method. The high-mounted fuselage offered the gunner sitting in the nose of the bow an excellent all-round view and very good defence possibilities. The pilot sitting behind the wing, however, had an obscured downward view. The aircraft was protected against enemy fire by a metal baffle on the front fuselage nose and on the engine nacelles. After the successful first flight on 30 January 1915, the prototype, designated as Friedel–Ursinus (FU), was accepted on 20 February 1915 in Darmstadt by Idflieg. An immediate mass production of the aircraft was recommended. After talks with various aircraft manufacturers such as Fokker and Flugzeugbau Friedrichshafen, Ursinus finally sold the licence of the aircraft in March 1915 to GWF, and Ursinus himself took over the construction supervision in the production programme. In order to make the aircraft even lighter and faster, the armour was not installed on the mass-produced aircraft. Starting in June 1915, the first versions of the aircraft, now known as the Gotha G I (G—large aircraft), were added to the Imperial German Flying Corps. The prototype, the FU, was used on the Eastern Front under the command of Major Friedel, who had been transferred there in late 1914 as a staff officer of the 'Flieger (Stofl) 9'. As intended, the aircraft flew as an armed escort for reconnaissance aircraft; later it was also used as a bomber. A Gotha G I was used together with some Fokker

With the construction of the Gotha G I by Oskar Ursinus in 1915, the development of Gotha large aircraft, the 'Gothas', began. (*DEHLA*)

Above and below: Rail transport: The aircraft built in Gotha were delivered in disassembled condition by rail—like this Gotha G I. (*DEHLA*)

Designer Oskar Ursinus himself (*left*) in the front. The weapon of the G I, was a 2-cm Becker cannon. (*DEHLA*)

single-seat fighters in the Sonderstaffel S 1 for the protection of the Ruhr area and stationed on the airfield Cologne-Butzweilerhof. This aircraft had been tentatively equipped with a 2-cm machine gun from Becker. Unfortunately, the reports on the effectiveness of this cannon, which was also installed on the marine biplane Gotha WD 7, have been lost. Due to the rapid technical development during this time, the G I was considered outdated in the middle of 1915. The aircraft were withdrawn from the front and delivered as school machines to flyer replacement departments. A total of 18 Gotha G Is were built.

Oskar Ursinus, Engineer, Journalist, 'Rhönvater'

Born in Weißenfels (Prussian province of Saxony) in 1877, the civil engineer was interested in aviation at an early age. Starting in 1908, Ursinus published the German aviation magazine *Flugsport: Illustrierte technische Zeitschrift und Anzeiger* (*Aviation: Illustrated technical Magazine and Gazette for all Aviation*). However, writing was not enough for him. In 1910, he became active himself and built his first aircraft, a monoplane with a 15-hp engine. In 1915, he founded large-scale aircraft construction in Gotha with the licensing of his twin-engined FU fighter aircraft to GWF. After the First World War, he made a name for himself as a patron of gliding in Germany. In his magazine, he printed out an invitation

Ursinus in front of a blackboard. (*DEHLA*)

for the first gliding competition in 1920. It was to take place on the Wasserkuppe, a 950-metre-high mountain in the Rhön. The popularity of this sport in Germany since then is mainly due to his efforts. From this point on, Ursinus has also been called 'Rhönvater'. He also tried to break new ground in the development of alternative movement drives. In 1935, for example, through the Muscle Flight Institute at the Frankfurt Polytechnic Society, he organised a competition for a self-made aircraft powered by muscle power. Ursinus's passion for flying rubbed off on his children. He had three sons who all became pilots. Two of them never returned from the Second World War. Oskar Ursinus died in Frankfurt am Main in 1952.

Gotha G II—Bomber

The licensed construction of Friedel-Ursinus's FU as Gotha G I was GWF's successful entry into the construction of large aircraft. Based on the Ursinus construction, the company specialised in the manufacture of twin-engined bombers. While the G I was being mass-produced in Gotha, Director-General Albert Kandt commissioned chief designer Hans Burkhard to develop a successor model as a long-range bomber that could carry a bombload of 300 kg, and as a result, at the beginning of 1916, the Gotha G II was created. Burkhard decided against Ursinus's concept of the overhead fuselage and constructed a conventional

The operational career of the Gotha G II was relatively short due to the unreliable engine Mercedes D.IV and led to the further development of the Gotha G III. (*DEHLA*)

At the end of August 1916, Romania entered the war on the side of the Allies. The 20th Squadron of Kampfgeschwader 4 with their Gotha G II pictured on the left. The squadron belonged to the mixed German bomber formation, which flew bombing raids against Romania from a Bulgarian airfield. (*Author's collection*)

biplane. The aircraft was powered by two eight-cylinder in-line Mercedes D.IV engines with 220 hp each designed as pusher propellers. The three-man crew consisted of a pilot, observer, and gunner, each with a machine gun pointing forwards and backwards. On 7 September 1915, GWF received the construction contract for three test aircraft from Idflieg, which was expanded to ten units three months later. The twin-bay prototype flew for the first time in March 1916, but did not reach the target height. Therefore the span was increased again and another bay was placed between the wings. The first three-bay series aircraft were then assigned to Kampfgeschwader 4 Staffel 20 in August 1916 and were used against Romania. However, after constant crankshaft breaks in the Mercedes engine, the aircraft had to be gradually withdrawn from use and so only a few flights were made on the front.

Gotha G III—Bomber

The Gotha G II became the further developed Gotha G III. This differed from the G II, except for the engine, only in small details and the slightly increased bombload. Hans Burkhard also reinforced the fuselage and built in a third machine gun that could shoot down and back through an opening in the floor of the fuselage, the so-called 'Gotha tunnel'. The aircraft was powered by two newly developed six-cylinder in-line Mercedes D.IVa engines with 260 hp each. On 3 May 1916, Idflieg ordered a total of 25 units with the military numbers G.375-399/16. Starting on 16 October 1916, with only two exceptions, the entire delivery block was delivered to Kampfgeschwader 2 der Obersten Heeresleitung (Tactical Bomber Wing of the German Army's High Command), 'Kagohl 2' for short, stationed on the Western Front, off Verdun. It was almost four months before a G III was shot down over France for the first time; during a mission on 8 February 1917 near St Mihiel, French fighter pilots Georges Guynemer and André Chainat of the Escadrille N.3 managed to bring down a Gotha G III. For Guynemer, it was the 31st and for Chainat the 11th aerial victory. The crew was able to make an emergency landing behind the enemy lines, but they were not able to set the aircraft on fire. The aircraft became the spoils of war and the crew was taken prisoner by the French. The British also succeeded in shooting down a G III in April 1917 and captured the aircraft almost completely undamaged. By the end of August 1917, the remaining Gotha G IIIs in the front units gave way to their successors. One machine was used by Daimler Motorengesellschaft (DMG) for testing purposes.

Gotha G IV—Long-Range Bomber

The development of the Gotha G II and G III showed the German military leadership the potential that these long-range bombers had. At the same time, it aroused the desire to improve these aircraft further and to replace the sluggish

The Gotha G III was an evolution of the G II with a Mercedes D.IVa engine. (*Stiftung Deutsches Technikmuseum Berlin*)

This postcard shows the wreck of the Gotha G III, G.377/16 of the 12th squadron of the KG 2, which was shot down near St Mihiel on 8 February 1917, as a war trophy in Nancy. The crew, NCO Werner Günther (pilot), Lieutenant Werner Schmid (observer), and gunner August Schwartz, were captured. Lieutenant Schmid was shot while trying to escape on 19 May 1917. (*Author's collection*)

and vulnerable Zeppelin airships that were used in the bombing of the United Kingdom. Therefore, on 4 August 1916, Idflieg ordered a successor to the G III with a higher speed, greater range, and larger bombload; as a consequence, 52 Gotha G IV bombers were ordered. GWF designer Hans Burkhard then developed the G III further into the G IV. The production of the new bomber took place in the GWF as well as under licence at the Siemens-Schuckert-Werken (SSW) and later also the Luft-Verkehrs-Gesellschaft AG (LVG) in the Pomeranian Köslin. To improve flight behaviour, the new model received ailerons on the lower wing. The fuselage was reinforced and covered with plywood. This was to allow the G IV to stay afloat for a short time in an emergency—an important prerequisite for attacks across the English Channel. As with the G III, the G IV also received the 'Gotha tunnel'. The aircraft was powered by two Mercedes D.IVa, each with 260 hp, which enabled the G IV to reach a maximum height of 5,000 metres and speed of 135 kph. GWF delivered the first two G IVs to the Kagohl 2 (Tactical Bomber Wings of the German Army's High Command) for testing in November 1916. Afterwards, there were improvement requests that had to be incorporated into the series production in Gotha. For example, GWF installed an additional tank in the upper wing of several G IVs, as the operational range was rated as insufficient. Due to these changes, there were production delays and the first series of G IVs were not available until March 1917. Two months later, the 'Kagohl 3' under the command of Captain Ernst Brandenburg (1883–1952), the so-called 'England Squadron' (after 18 December 1917 renamed to 'Bogohl 3' (Bomber Wings of the German Army's High Command)), was ready for action. Under the codename 'Operation Turkish Cross', the squadron began designated strategic bombing raids on London. On 25 May 1917, 23 Gotha G IVs took off for the first daytime attack on London. The target was overcast, however, so the bombers attacked alternative targets on the Channel coast. Two G IVs were lost in the attack, and one of them was shot down by British fighters on the return flight. On 13 June 1917 at 10 a.m., 22 Gothas with 200 kg of bombs each took off from the Belgian airfields Gontrode and St Denis near Ghent for the next attempt on London. Five aircraft had to turn around before reaching their destination due to technical problems. The remaining 17 G IVs penetrated the centre of London relatively unhindered and were able to release their bomb payload there. The horrible balance was of 162 dead, including 18 children in a school. Another 432 people were injured. The outcry from the British public was huge: Bombers from Gotha over the inner city of London and in Buckingham Palace, a German-born royal family with the name Sachsun-Coburg und Gotha! The public pressure became so great that the royal family rid themselves of all German titles and renamed the family 'Windsor'. In addition, Parliament passed a law according to which, in January 1919, King George V of Great Britain and Ireland had to deprive his German cousin, Duke Carl Eduard von Sachsen-Coburg und Gotha, of all English nobility titles. With this, the Windsors finally and officially cut all of their family ties to Gotha.

A total of 232 Gotha G IVs were built by GWF and the licensees LVG and SSW. The Austro-Hungarian Kaiserliche und Königliche Luftfahrtruppen (K.u.K.

For the first time for a type of aircraft from Gotha, licensees were also involved in the large-scale production of Gotha G IV. The Kagohl 3 'England Squadron' was exclusively equipped with the G IV. (*Gotha City Archives, signature 6.1/1417 image 25*)

Parade formation of the 'England Squadron', equipped with Gotha G IV. The squadron flew daytime raids on England from Gontrode and St Denis in occupied Belgium from May to August 1917. (*DEHLA*)

Luftfahrtruppen) ordered 40 Gotha G IVs; this batch was built at the beginning of 1918 under licence from LVG in Köslin. In contrast to the German aircraft, they were equipped with two 230-hp Hiero engines. The engines were a constant nuisance as they were prone to frequent failures. This was due to structural defects on the engine mounts and propellers which created strong vibrations. The aircraft remained on the ground until the cause of the engine problems was identified and resolved, and as a consequence the G IVs flew only a few missions.

Hans Burkhard

Hans Burkhard was born in Winterthur, Switzerland, in 1888. In 1908, Burkhard, who was studying at the technical centre in Burgdorf, turned to aircraft construction and moved to the engineering school in Mainz, Germany. His first self-constructed aircraft was a biplane with a 22-hp Anzani engine. In February 1911, his attempts to take off on the frozen lake of St Moritz failed because the engine turned out to be too weak. A few months later he obtained his licence from the aircraft manufacturer Nieuport in France, and at the same time his career as an aircraft designer began. At the end of 1911, Burkhard was employed by Edmund Rumpler in his company in Berlin, but the two soon fell out. After their differences drove them apart, Burkhard placed an advertisement in the magazine *Flugsport*. Through this advertisement, the Deutsche Bristol-Werke in Halberstadt, which later became Halberstädter Flugzeugwerke GmbH, became aware of him and hired him. In September 1914, he became acquainted with Karl Caspar, who recommended that he apply to GWF. Director-General Albert Kandt, who was still looking for a capable designer, was able to convince Burkhard to move to Gotha. Burkhard took over the land aircraft construction department and immediately began construction of the Gotha LD 5 cavalry aircraft, an armed, single-engined biplane. He achieved his greatest success in early 1916 with the twin-engined Gotha G II aircraft and the further improved successor types G III, G IV, and G V. This made GWF one of the largest and most important German aircraft manufacturers. Burkhard is also considered to be the inventor of the so-called 'Gotha tunnel', which was a firing channel in the rear part of the fuselage, with which a defence to the rear and downwards was possible without an additional mounted machine gun. In 1917, he designed the Gotha G VI, the world's first asymmetrical aircraft. However, Burkhard did not manage to get this machine ready for series production. Afterwards, he worked on his last project at the GWF—the Gotha GL X, a light twin-engined combat and image reconnaissance aircraft based on the G VII and G VIII designed by Rösner and Schleiffer. After the Armistice in 1918 and the temporary end of aircraft construction, Burkhard's collaboration with the Gothaer Waggonfabrik ended. After a brief interlude at Junkers, he returned to his home in Switzerland in 1921. Until his retirement in 1946, he worked there in various functions for the local flying corps, his last position was as an operations engineer for the army aviation park in Dübendorf. Hans Burkhard died in 1977.

The Swiss designer Hans Burkhard in front of the Gotha G II which he designed. (*DEHLA*)

Gotha G V, G Va, G Vb—Bombers

The Gotha G V was a further development of the G IV. Hans Burkhard began the design work in the autumn of 1916. The dimensions remained the same as its predecessor model, the Gotha G IV. The engines—two Mercedes D.IVas—were identical. However, Burkhard changed the way the engines were mounted between the wings. The tanks of the G IV were under the engines, which meant that in an emergency landing with a broken chassis, the tanks were crushed and could easily catch fire. In the case of the G V, the tanks were moved into the reinforced fuselage. The weight of the new bomber increased by 170 kg, which had a negative effect on flight performance and was therefore no improvement. The first completed G V reached the 'England Squadron' in September 1917, just at the moment when the squadron stopped the heavy-loss daytime raids against England. The G Vs then used for the following night operations also incurred losses, less from the enemy, but more from crash landings at night. Most of the time, the over-tired crews overturned their planes on landing. As a remedy, a push chassis was installed to prevent rollover. To do this, the technicians built another landing gear in front of the fuselage bow. In addition, the aircraft designated as Gotha G Va received a tail unit similar to a biplane, the so-called box tail unit, which was supposed to improve single-engined flight. Twenty-five G Vas were built and delivered to Bogohl 3 commencing April 1918. The further developed Gotha G Vb also had a box tail, though the chassis under the bow was omitted. For this purpose, the undercarriage under the wings was given a second pair of

The prototype of the Gotha G V on the GWF airfield. (*Krieg collection*)

Through an opening in the bottom of the fuselage, the 'Gotha tunnel', the gunner was also able to repel enemy aircraft approaching from below. The shock chassis on the bow of this G Va should prevent a rollover on landing. (*DEHLA*)

Long-range bomber Gotha G Vb with a front bumper under the wings and box tail for improved single-engined flight. (*Gotha City Archives, signature 6.1/1417 image 26*)

wheels in front as a push undercarriage. These measures again increased the curb weight of the aircraft and once again worsened flight performance, especially at peak altitude. The Gotha G Vbs, which were delivered in October 1918, were no longer used against England. The last of a total of 15 night missions against England was flown on the night of 19–20 May 1918. After that, the Bogohl 3 was used on the Western Front against French targets behind enemy lines and to support the last German ground offensives of the war. A total of 205 Gotha G Vs, G Vas, and G Vbs are said to have been built.

Gotha G VI—Experimental Aircraft

The Gotha G VI designed by Hans Burkhard was the first asymmetrical aircraft in the world. In an interview with a Swiss newspaper in 1942, Burkhard replied to the question of how he came up with the idea for the aircraft: 'The Gothas (the twin-engined G II–G V bombers) offered the air three resistance bodies.... I pondered whether the number of these air resistances could not be reduced. It worked … with the absurd idea of asymmetry. This is how the Gotha G VI came about.'[2] Burkhard had the idea for this solution as early as 1915 when he designed a successor to the Gotha G I designed by Oskar Ursinus for GWF. First, a conventional biplane, the Gotha G II, was implemented. Burkhard patented the idea for the asymmetrical aircraft in various designs in 1915 and 1916. When the Imperial German Flying Corps demanded improved long-range bombers with higher speeds and higher altitudes from the industry for use against England a year later, Burkhard pulled his patent out of the drawer and designed the asymmetrical Gotha G VI. Burkhard relied on tried and tested elements from the G II to V series for the design. The basis of the new aircraft was the fuselage of a Gotha G IV, which received a Mercedes D.IVa with a pull propeller up front. The fuselage had a simple tail assembly with a defensive stand to the rear. There was a second, short fuselage set one propeller length to the right of the main fuselage. It offered a defensive stand facing forward and a Mercedes D.IVa with a pusher propeller to the rear. With this design, Burkhard wanted to kill several birds with one stone: With only two drag bodies, the air resistance should be reduced while increasing the speed. In addition, there were improved visibility and defence options. When the unusual-looking aircraft was finished in late 1917/early 1918, no GWF works pilot wanted to fly it. Burkhard was only able to win over FEA 3 pilots for the maiden flight 'only after a lot of persuasion'. There are even said to have been bets among the GWF employees whether the plane could actually fly straight ahead or only in a circle. But the G VI flew. During the test flight, the pilots noticed vibrations at the end of the fuselage, presumably caused by the propeller flow over the motor nacelle.[4] Those who flew the aircraft were Leutnant d.R. Hauff and the graduate engineer Michael Schleiffer, along with Karl Rösner designer of the Gotha GL VII/G VIII. The unusual appearance of the aircraft also caused a sensation among the citizens of Gotha. During the test flights over the city, there were several phone calls to GWF from people reporting frantically

Crash landing of a Gotha G VI. The unusual design of the asymmetrical aircraft is clearly visible. (*Stiftung Deutsches Technikmuseum Berlin*)

about an aircraft that had lost an engine. The G VI was badly damaged in a crash landing in the spring of 1918. Various sources report of a second G VI, which was subsequently tested and apparently also damaged in the process. In any case, the repair of the aircraft and the elimination of the problems with the vibrations at the end of the fuselage dragged on until the end of the war. In addition, the GWF's focus was now more on the GL VII/GL VIII developed in parallel by Karl Rösner, and Burkhard was later busy designing the GL X. New test flights with the G VI therefore no longer took place. To make sure that the unusual construction did not become spoils of the war, GWF had the aircraft destroyed by burning shortly after the Armistice.

Gotha GL VII/G VII—Reconnaissance Aircraft, Bomber

Shortly after the introduction of the Gotha G IV and G V, the air force demanded significantly more powerful bombers. The new 'lightened' large aircraft of the GL type should reach at least 180 kph at an altitude of 4,000 to 6,000 metres. Idflieg demanded a 'photography special' aircraft that could perform all imaging tasks for long-range and close-up reconnaissance, situational target exploration, and a machine that could carry all imaging equipment. This would be made possible by a special high-altitude engine, the six-cylinder Maybach Mb.IVa in-line engine. GWF took part in the bidding, and Karl Rösner—the technical director of the entire aircraft construction department at GWF in 1917—then designed, with help from the ideas and patents of the designer Dipl.-Ing. Michael Schleiffer, a completely new type of bomber. The difference from the predecessor models that Hans Burkhard had designed was not only skin deep. The composite biplane consisted of a plywood-clad fuselage and an aerodynamically clad nose. There was only room for two crew members in the fuselage, the pilot in front and the observer behind. Rösner decided against a front machine-gun position. For defence, the pilot would receive a forward-firing, rigid machine gun. The two aerodynamically faired engines were arranged close to the longitudinal axis of the fuselage so that the two propeller circles almost touched each other. This was done to improve the single-engined flight and manoeuvrability of the aircraft. Two versions were created, the twin-bay and later three-bay version was designated as GL VII, and the enlarged, three-and-a-half-bay version as Gotha GL VIII. In September 1917, GWF presented the two test aircraft to Idflieg. The top speed of the GL VII was 180 kph. With these promising achievements, Idflieg immediately ordered series production. A total of 355 G VIIs and G VIIIs were commissioned; 55 of them were to be built in Gotha, 100 more under licence at Aviatik in Leipzig, and 200 at LVG in Köslin. But before the GL VII went into production as the G VII, GWF had to get the most out of the design, especially with regard to the high-altitude flight characteristics. The company worked closely with Idflieg, which sent its own specialists to Gotha for this purpose. Four pre-series aircraft were built (G.550/17 to 553/17), which differed in the wingspan, the tail unit, the engine, and the type of propeller. The test results should immediately flow into series production. However, the tests and several crash landings of the four test types delayed the construction programme, so the series production started very slowly. For example, one of the first pre-series GL VII had a simple vertical tail, but the series aircraft received a box tail. Up to 30 Gotha G VIIs with Mercedes D.IVas are said to have been built by Aviatik by the end of the war. At GWF, the series aircraft apparently retained the designation GL VII and were equipped with the heavy Maybach Mb.IVa engine. Why they are called GL VII on the one hand and then G VII on the other can no longer be clarified. The sources that have survived do not provide a clear answer to this question. Eight aircraft designated as GL VII are said to have been built in Gotha, three of which were taken over by Czechoslovakia after the Armistice in 1918. On the way to Prague, however, the aircraft were confiscated by the French after an emergency landing. The British took over five Gotha G VIIs from aviation production in Cologne-Butzweilerhof. During the transfer to Abbeville, the G VII (Av) G.105/18 crashed on 9 January 1919 four miles south-east of the city of Monschau. Royal Air Force Lieutenant John Harrison Gardiner and Second Lieutenant James Wood from No. 100 Squadron were killed.

Gotha G VIII—Bomber

The Gotha G VIII was based on the test type Gotha GL VIII. While this was still powered by two six-cylinder in-line Mercedes D.IVa engines, the large-scale version called G VIII was to be equipped with two Maybach Mb.IVa high-altitude engines. In terms of construction, the G VIII was the enlarged version of the Gotha G VII, which was developed in parallel. The fuselage was slightly longer and the wingspan of the three-and-a-half-bay biplane was larger, but only a few G VIIIs were completed by the end of the war. One of them was still under construction in Gotha in November 1918. Rösner recalled in an interview that this aircraft was bought by Ukraine after the Armistice. During the transfer, the aircraft was presumably confiscated by Czechoslovakia during an emergency landing in Bratislava. What happened to the aircraft is not known.

Gotha G IX (LVG)—Bomber

The Gotha G IX (LVG) is a further development of the G VIII as a high-altitude bomber with an even larger wingspan. Like the G VIII, the aircraft was powered by two Maybach Mb.IVa engines and was intended to replace the Gotha G V in the Bogohl 3. In total, Idflieg ordered 170 machines, and those that were actually built under this order were produced exclusively under licence by LVG in Köslin. Around 90 G IX (LVG) aircraft are said to have been built by the end of the war; some of these, which had stopped at the last aerodrome of the Bogohl 3 in Brussels-Evere, were taken over by the Belgian Air Force. About 30 Gotha G IX

Four pre-series aircraft were built from the Gotha GL VII with the Mercedes D.IVa. All with different engines, spans, and tail units. (*Author's collection*)

Gotha GL VII G.304/18 with box tail unit manufactured at GWF. The photograph shows the aircraft at FEA 14 in Halle/Saale in November 1918. Sitting in a flying suit on the plane, Dipl.-Ing. Michael Schleiffer, after whose ideas and patents the G VII/G VIII series was created. (*DEHLA*)

The three-and-a-half-bay high-altitude bomber Gotha G VIII was to replace the Gotha G V. (*Author's collection*)

The Gotha G IX (LVG) bomber was built exclusively by LVG. (*Stiftung Deutsches Technikmuseum Berlin*)

were handed over to the British at the central collection point, the Cologne-Butzweilerhof airfield. During the transfer to England, the G.257/18 had an accident shortly after take-off. The two lieutenants, Leonard Stanley Hewitt and Beavan Carlton-Smith of No. 100 Squadron, died in the accident.

Gotha GL X—Reconnaissance and Attack Aircraft

The Gotha GL X was considered the highlight of GWF's large aircraft development. Idflieg ordered three machines of the new type on 16 August 1918. Two different versions were to be created. On the one hand a fast, high-flying reconnaissance aircraft, on the other hand an attack aircraft that was to be equipped with a 2-cm Becker cannon and several forward-firing machine guns. Hans Burkhard used the Gotha G VII/G VIII series as the basis for the construction of the GL X. The aircraft was powered by two BMW IIIa six-cylinder in-line engines with 185 hp each. An unarmed prototype was completed in January 1919. It is not known whether there were any test flights. Presumably the prototype had to be scrapped after the arrival of the Inter-Allied Military Control Commission in Gotha.

Gotha GL X. The photograph was probably taken shortly after the prototype was completed in early 1919. To the right of it is a Gotha WD 27. (*Gotha City Archives, signature 6.1/1417 image 36*)

Friedrichshafen G IVa—Bomber

Since the Gotha designers did not succeed in putting the promising Gotha G VII and G VIII into series production, GWF received an order from Idflieg on 21 August 1918 to build 50 Friedrichshafen G IVa bombers under licence. The four-bay biplane could carry a bombload of 1,000 kg and was powered by two Mercedes D.IVa engines, each producing 260 hp. Almost three months later, the guns were idle: none of these planes were completed in Gotha.

Competing under licence: On 21 August 1918, Idflieg commissioned GWF to replicate the Friedrichshafen G IVa, the design of which the former Gotha-based designer Karl Grulich had also been involved in. (*Mückler collection*)

4

VGO—Giant Aircraft from Gotha-East

The 'Gothas' were not the only large aircraft that were built in Gotha. At the end of August 1914, by agreement, the VGO company settled on the grounds of the Gothaer Waggonfabrik and erected a large hall in order to build giant aircraft. The GWF provided the company with offices and a carpentry workshop, and 112 workers, 19 office staff, and 8 technicians were employed there at the beginning of 1916. VGO stood for Versuchsbau Gotha-Ost, a joint venture between the two Württemberg companies, Zeppelin and Robert Bosch. The chief designer was Professor Alexander Baumann, whom Gustav Klein, the entrepreneur behind the VGO, was able to poach from the Technical University of Stuttgart. Baumann (1875–1928) held what is probably the world's first chair for aeronautical engineering. With up to six engines and a wingspan of 42 metres for the largest model, these machines were even larger than the later large aircraft of the GWF. On 11 April 1915, VGO I, the first giant aircraft, took off. The aircraft, which was rebuilt after several crash landings, was taken over by the navy and designated as RML I (Reichs-Marine-Landflugzeug). The test models VGO II and III were produced in Gotha by August 1916, and were subsequently put into service by the air force. A fourth giant aircraft was already under construction. On 1 August 1916, the company moved to Staaken, in Berlin, after it had become too cramped in Gotha. The move was accompanied by a name change to Flugzeugwerft GmbH in Staaken. GWF bought the hall in Gotha from VGO in May 1917. The giant R IV aircraft, which was still completed in Gotha, had its maiden flight on 16 September 1916; however, it was not accepted by the military until 8 May 1917. At this point, the last employees who were still working on the giant aircraft left Gotha and moved to Berlin. The giant multi-engined aircraft built there, and then also under licence from other companies, were brought by Idflieg to the Riesen-Flugzeug-Abteilungen (Giant Aircraft Departments) (RFA) 500 and 501, which had been set up in 1916. Until May 1918, Staaken giant aircraft were used almost exclusively against England, or against the recommended alternative destinations along the French coast, including Dunkirk, Le Havre, and Calais. The Staaken often flew their night missions together with the Gotha bombers. Called 'Super-Gothas' by the British press, these aircraft no longer had anything to do with Gotha.

Giant VGO I aircraft next to Gotha LD 5 cavalry aircraft, taken in the spring of 1915 at the Gotha factory airfield (*DEHLA*)

The giant aircraft VGO II was a further development of the VGO I and had its first flight in Gotha at the beginning of September 1915. (*DEHLA*)

5

Gotha Seaplanes

The history of Gotha seaplanes began in April 1913 with the construction of a seaplane developed by Bruno Büchner. Five months later, the Austrian-Hungarian designer Karl Rösner moved from Albatros Flugzeugwerke in Johannistal near Berlin to Gotha. There he was hired on 1 September 1913 as chief designer for the still young section of seaplane construction. His assistant was engineer Albrecht Klaube. Gotha is 500 kilometres inland from the sea and there are no large lakes in the vicinity that could be used as test areas. To overcome this problem GWF built a concrete water basin adjacent to the airfield. At least the buoyancy of the aircraft could then be tested. For testing at sea, GWF established a branch in Warnemünde on the Baltic Sea. The aircraft were manufactured in Gotha, then dismantled and transported to Warnemünde by rail. There they were put together again in an assembly hall, but the hall was barely finished in the summer of 1914 when the First World War broke out. The Imperial German Navy immediately confiscated the GWF hall and set up its Seaplane Testing Command—*Seeflugzeug Versuchs Kommando* (SVK)—there. The SVK had a special key function between the client *Reichsmarineamt* (RMA), the aircraft manufacturers, and the two naval seaplane departments as buyers. All of the seaplanes that the RMA commissioned from the German aircraft industry were first tested in Warnemünde before they were handed over to the navy. Since GWF no longer had the opportunity to test its aircraft itself after the navy took over its branch, this role fell to the SVK. The SVK not only influenced the technical development of all German seaplanes, but also drove them forward. The command was also responsible for testing new equipment in the aircraft, such as radios or on-board weapons, thus stimulating the industry to come up with innovative ideas. The activity reports, which the SVK had to submit to the RMA every two weeks, show this influence very well—especially with regard to the development of the Gotha torpedo aircraft. The positive assessment by the SVK played a decisive role in the GWF becoming the preferred manufacturer of these aircraft.

Production of torpedo planes Gotha WD 11 at GWF. (*Author's collection*)

Seaplane Büchner—Competition Aircraft

The seaplane built by GWF for Bruno Büchner in April 1913 was a biplane with a lattice fuselage, two floats, and a 100-hp Mercedes engine designed with a pusher propeller. Production started relatively quickly. Büchner presumably had the design documents with him when he came to Gotha in early 1913. This is probably why Büchner's seaplane—like the land biplane that was built at the same time—was never officially considered a GWF in-house construction. As early as the end of June 1913, Büchner wanted to compete in a seaplane competition on Lake Constance but he fell ill shortly before and was not able to participate. Information about flight characteristics and whereabouts of the machine have not been handed down. Büchner left Gotha and was recruited as a pilot for Bulgaria in the First Balkan War against the Ottoman Empire. Later, he went to the colony of German South West Africa (today Namibia) as a mail pilot. At the beginning of the First World War, he piloted a Pfalz-built Otto B. pusher biplane that had been converted into a seaplane and flew reconnaissance for the Imperial Protection Force in German East Africa (now Tanzania). Here Büchner was taken prisoner by the British and was only released after the war. Büchner died in Austria on 30 November 1943.

The Büchner seaplane. The first seaplane built in Gotha was created two months after the aircraft department was founded based on plans by Bruno Büchner. (*Gotha City Archives, signature 6.1/1417 image 2*)

Gotha WD 1—Sea Reconnaissance Aircraft

After the unsuccessful experiment with the Büchner seaplane, GWF looked around for a tried and tested aircraft design. This was to be used as the basis for future in-house developments. In the summer of 1913, the Imperial German Navy had acquired the prototype of the single-engined seaplane Avro 503 made by the British manufacturer A. V. Roe & Company Ltd. The two-seater biplane was equipped with a nine-cylinder 100-hp Gnome rotary engine. The float system consisted of a tail float and two cushioned floats under the wings, which were designed in such a way that they could also absorb hard shocks on rough seas. After the Imperial German Navy had successfully completed tests on the North Sea, GWF also became aware of the model. GWF acquired the licence for the aircraft from Avro and the Gotha replica was named Gotha WD 1 (*Wasser Doppeldecker*—water biplane) and was, apart from small details, an identical copy of the Avro 503. In December 1913, the Gotha version was transported to Warnemünde for testing on the Baltic Sea. This began in February 1914. On 4 April 1914, Heinrich Dahm and a passenger carried out the first German overseas flight from Warnemünde to Gedser in Denmark, 45 km away. The flight was not without complications: when Dahm was circling the Warnemünde-Gedser ferry, a valve broke on the engine, forcing him to float on the Baltic Sea; although the sea was rough, he managed to 'undertake the repair with the spare parts on board and continue the flight', reported German magazine *Flugsport*. Presumably this incident was the reason for installing a different engine. The aircraft, modified with a six-cylinder in-line Mercedes D.I engine, was designated Gotha WD 1a. With this aircraft,

The first Gotha seaplane, the Gotha WD 1, was built under licence from the British Avro 503. (*Gotha City Archives, signature 6.1/1418 image 8*)

With one passenger on board, Heinrich Dahm made the first overseas flight of a German aircraft from Warnemünde to Gedser in Denmark in a Gotha WD 1 on 4 April 1914. He needed 32 minutes for the 45-km route. It was a pioneering achievement at the time. Four years later, multi-engined long-range reconnaissance planes of the WD series were underway on up to eight-hour reconnaissance flights over the sea. (*DEHLA*)

GWF wanted to take part in a seaplane competition that was due to take place in Warnemünde from 1–10 August 1914, but with the onset of war, it was cancelled. With German mobilisation in early August 1914, the Imperial German Navy took over all aircraft that were registered for the competition. The Gotha WD 1a received the Marine number 59 and was transferred to Kiel. On 14 December 1914, the navy bought five more Gotha WD 1as, equipped with the Mercedes D.I engine, which GWF delivered with the Marine numbers 285 to 289 in early 1915. The unarmed aircraft were used by the Imperial German Navy as reconnaissance aircraft for patrol flights along the coast and as training aircraft. In June 1915, the navy gave away three WD 1as and then in September two more WD 1as to the Ottoman Empire, which used the aircraft with German crews for reconnaissance over the Aegean and Black Seas.

Gotha WD 2—Sea Reconnaissance Aircraft

Based on the Gotha WD 1, the Gotha WD 2 designed by Karl Rösner was the first independent Gotha seaplane. The two-seater biplane formed the basis of a whole family of single-engined reconnaissance aircraft for the navy, which were constantly being improved upon. For the competition in Warnemünde, two WD 2s were built, one with a 150-hp Rapp engine and one with a 100-hp Mercedes D.I. Like the WD 1a, both machines were taken over in early August 1914 by the Imperial German Navy with the Marine numbers 60 and 61. In the same month, the *Reichs-Marine-Amt* ordered five more WD 2s in Gotha. The aircraft with the marine numbers 254–258 were shipped starting on 24 December 1914. These and all other Gotha WD 2 were powered by a 150-hp Benz Bz III engine. On 25 March 1915, another seven WD 2 (Marine numbers 236–240 and 424 and 425) were ordered from Gotha. The Ottoman Empire took over two machines from this lot. The WD 2 delivered to the Imperial German Navy were all unarmed. In contrast, the machines intended for the Turks were given a ring-mounted machine gun above the upper wing. For the overland transfer of the aircraft, a pair of wheels was installed under the float so that it could take off and land from solid ground. In several stages, the aircraft were transferred via Hungary, Serbia and Bulgaria to the Bosphorus, where the Turks were eagerly awaiting the aircraft. The Gotha WD 2 flew armed reconnaissance with German crews during the Allied landing operation near Gallipolli. By mid-1916, GWF had built a total of 27 Gotha WD 2s in several production batches, from which the Turks received at least ten machines.

Stress test on a Gotha WD 2 for the Ottoman Empire. The fourth from the left next to the three gentlemen of the Turkish acceptance commission is Karl Rösner, the designer of the WD 2. The water basin still exists today, but is only used as a fire extinguishing pond. (*DEHLA*)

A total of 27 Gotha WD 2s were built. The WD 2 with the Marine number 424 was probably delivered to the Ottoman Empire. (*Gotha City Archives, signature 6.1/1418 image 14*)

Karl Rösner

Karl Rösner was born in Mährisch Schönberg (now Šumperk in the Czech Republic) in the Austro-Hungarian Empire in 1880 and studied mechanical engineering in Vienna. He gained his first experience in aircraft construction at Rumpler in Berlin, where he became an employee on 2 February 1909. A year later, he designed his first aircraft, a monoplane. With this aircraft, he took part in the 'German round-trip flight for the B.Z. Prize of the Air 1911' and won the first additional award for non-pilots and designers. The dream of his own aircraft factory was not to be realised and instead he accepted an offer to work as chief designer at the aircraft manufacturer Albatros. He started in Johannisthal on 12 May 1913. A flying boat was built there on behalf of the Reich Marine Office, and Rösner was involved in its construction. To save space, the aircraft had folding wings, a design feature that Rösner later also applied to the Gotha WD 14. On 1 September 1913, he moved to the seaplane construction department in Gotha as chief designer and, until Hans Burkhard joined the company on 1 October 1914, he was also responsible for the construction of land aircraft. From 1917 until the end of aircraft construction in the autumn of 1920, he was the technical director of the entire department. Then Rösner returned to his homeland and became the technical director at the Czechoslovakian aircraft manufacturer Aero in Prague. Via Yugoslavia, Rösner moved to Fieseler in Kassel in early 1934, before returning to GWF in May 1936. Here, among other things, he was responsible for the licensed construction of the Gotha Go 145. Karl Rösner died after a serious illness in Ruma (Croatia) in 1942.

The Austrian-Hungarian designer Karl Rösner was employed by GWF from 1913 to 1910 and again from 1936 until his death in 1942. (*Author's collection*)

Gotha WD 3—Sea Reconnaissance Aircraft

In August 1914, Karl Rösner began building the experimental aircraft Gotha WD 3, an armed two-seater biplane with a pusher propeller made entirely of wood, on behalf of the RMA. The new part about the design was the short central fuselage on the lower wing, which accommodated the two-man crew with a six-cylinder in-line Mercedes D.III engine with 160 hp. The tail assembly was connected to the lower wing by two lens-shaped tail assembly supports. As the propeller was attached to the rear of the fuselage, the observer seated in front of the pilot did not have to cope with exhaust gases or turbulence and had a clear field of fire. In addition to the machine gun pointing forward, the observer also operated a radio. The construction of this experimental aircraft was obviously not a high priority. Only on 14 September 1915 was the prototype registered with the Marine number 259 and handed over to the SVK in Warnemünde. The tests showed that the WD 3 was relatively heavy (despite its lightweight construction) and only had moderate flight performance. Further construction in this form was therefore rejected. The only aircraft built remained in Warnemünde and is said to have been used by the SVK as a training aircraft. According to other sources, the aircraft is said to have been converted to the Gotha WD 2. There were, however, no references to this in the official documents. Considering the effort that would be required to do this conversion, it seems rather unlikely.

The Gotha WD 3 twin-fuselage aircraft on the GWF water basin in Gotha. (*Gotha City Archives, signature 6.1/1418 image 12*)

Gotha UWD—Sea Reconnaissance Aircraft, Bomber

The Gotha UWD (*Ursinus Wasser Doppeldecker*, Ursinus water biplane) was the seaplane version of the FU. The RMA ordered a unit in Gotha in April 1915. GWF referred to the aircraft internally as Gotha WD 4. The aircraft was powered by two six-cylinder in-line Mercedes D.III engines with 160 hp each. On 30 December 1915, the unique piece with the Marine number 120 was handed over to the SVK in Warnemünde. The first test flights on the Baltic Sea began on 5 January 1916. A month later, the Imperial German Navy took over the aircraft and stationed it at the Zeebrugge sea flight station in occupied Belgium. From here, the naval aviators used the aircraft for several successful missions against the British. One such flight took place on 19 March 1916, when 120 attacked the port facilities of Dover in conjunction with other German aircraft. On 10 July 1916, the UWD was so badly damaged during a hard landing on the water that it was not worth repairing and the aircraft was written-off.

Gotha WD 5—Sea Reconnaissance Aircraft

On 24 April 1915, the RMA ordered a small, high-speed reconnaissance aircraft from GWF, which should also be able to carry bombs. Rösner then designed the Gotha WD 5, a two-seater biplane, with a 160-hp Mercedes D.III in-line engine. On 7 August 1915, the prototype with the Marine number 118 was handed over to the SVK. During the test, there were flutter phenomena on the tail assembly, which made it difficult to drop a targeted bomb. Presumably for this reason, there was only one aircraft built. The aircraft then served Captain Walter Langfeld, the commander of the Kiel-Holtenau sea flight station, as a personal service aircraft. After his assignment to the German naval aviators in Turkey in July 1916, he took the plane to the Bosphorus.

Hansa-Brandenburg NW (Gotha WD 6)—Sea Reconnaissance Aircraft

Since GWF had available production capacity at the beginning of 1916, the RMA awarded the licensed production of 30 single-engined sea reconnaissance aircraft Hansa-Brandenburg NW to GWF on 20 May 1916. The licence building is said to have been internally designated as Gotha WD 6 by GWF. The aircraft was a two-seater, unarmed biplane with floats, powered by a 160-hp Mercedes D.III engine. The first machine from Gothaer licence production received the Marine number 752 and was delivered to the SVK on 29 September 1916. However, before further aircraft could be handed over to the Marine, GWF had to make improvements. During the first trials at the beginning of October 1916, the SVK inspection officers found some deficiencies:

Above and below: The Gotha UWD after its completion at GWF. The plane was the FU's seaplane version. (*DEHLA*)

The Gotha WD 5 on the water basin in Gotha. The plane remained a one-off. (*Author's collection*)

A total of 30 Hansa-Brandenburg NW built by GWF under licence in 1916. (*Dr Koos collection*)

> Model specific aircraft in-flight testing…. Climbing performance with acceptance load: 800 m –8, 1000 m –10, 1500 m –16.5, 2000 m –29 , Speed –120 kph. The machine is extremely tail-heavy, when the bombs are attached, about 50 kg/m of reverse rotation are required to lift the machine.

The same case occurred with the second machine delivered. The delivery of the series had therefore stopped, director Ernst Heinkel (1888–1958, then technical director and chief designer at Hansa-Brandenburg—d.A.) and GWF designer Hans Rösner 'have been ordered to Warnemünde to determine the necessary remedy.' Another flight test activity could not take place because of the bad weather.[3] Two weeks later, the deficiencies were corrected:

> After changing the position of the floats, the tail-heaviness has been eliminated. The corresponding conversion has been commissioned for the entire series. The series is then to be delivered.[4]

With the handover of the last Hansa-Brandenburg NW built in Gotha to the SVK on 21 February 1917, the series was completed. The aircraft with the Marine numbers 752 to 781 were used by the Imperial German Navy as sea reconnaissance aircraft.

Gotha WD 7—Sea Reconnaissance Aircraft, Bomber

The Gotha WD 7 was the first large twin-engined aircraft of the Imperial German Navy to be procured in small series and was commissioned by the RMA in Gotha in February 1915—before the Gotha UWD, but after it had become aware of GWF's large aircraft development. The navy wanted to acquire torpedo bombers in the long term. A first step in this direction was the development of a twin-engined bomber and a maritime patrol aircraft. The RMA assumed that with the limited performance of the available German aircraft engines, only a twin-engined aircraft would be able to carry a torpedo and a two-person crew to the target. The most powerful German aircraft engines at that time only had a maximum output of 160 hp. Even with two 160-hp engines, the planes were underpowered. In addition to GWF, the Friedrichshafen, Albatros, and Hansa-Brandenburg aircraft plants also received the order to construct a twin-engined naval bomber. Karl Rösner then designed a water biplane (WD) with two Mercedes D.IIs with 120 hp each. In order to be able to fight enemy aircraft, a machine gun was installed in the fuselage nose, which was operated by the observer. At the beginning of 1916, the prototype of the Gotha WD 7, which was given Marine number 119, was tested at SVK in Warnemünde. Since the tests were very promising, the RMA ordered seven more Gotha WD 7s, which were equipped with either 120-hp Argus As.IIs or 100-hp Mercedes D.Is. The 119 was relocated to Zeebrugge, flew its first mission over the North Sea from there on 3 April 1916, and was immediately lost. Presumably, after

Gotha WD 7, Marine number 119. During its first use on 3 April 1916, the aircraft had to make an emergency landing over the North Sea. The 119 was damaged and captured by the French, the *Flugmeister* Kaspar and *Flugmeister* Rund were taken prisoner. (*Author's collection*)

taking on enemy fire, one of the engines caught fire and the crew had to make an emergency landing with the aircraft. When a French torpedo boat approached, the *Flugmeister* (petty officers) Rund and Kaspar jumped into the sea. The French were able to recover the damaged aircraft, and Rund and Kaspar were captured. The seven series aircraft with the Marine numbers 670 to 676 were mainly used as training aircraft for torpedo aircraft crews at the special command in Flensburg. The last two units produced with the Marine numbers 675 and 676 were retained by the SVK for testing the 2-cm Becker automatic cannon and were converted at the bow for this purpose. However, according to the SVK activity report of 5 December 1916, only the 676 was ultimately used for this. Test results with this weapon, which was also tested on the Gotha G I, have not been made available.

Gotha WD 8—Sea Reconnaissance Aircraft

The Gotha WD 8, Marine no. 476, was the single-engined variant of the Gotha WD 7. The dimensions of the machines were identical. The RMA only wanted to determine whether the same flight characteristics could be achieved with a more powerful engine as with the twin-engined WD 7. This comparison aircraft was commissioned in April 1915 and delivered in December 1915. In contrast to the WD 7, however, it was equipped with a six-cylinder in-line Maybach Mb.IVa engine with 240 hp. The aircraft was armed with two machine guns: one that could shoot forward, synchronized through the propeller, and a second that shot backwards to defend. The first tests at the SVK took place from February 1916. It was found that the single-engined WD 8 had similar flight performance as the twin-engined WD 7. The aircraft was then handed over to the Zeebrugge sea flight station together with the first WD 7 and was to be tested there under frontline conditions. Since the WD 7 was lost on the first flight against the enemy, a direct comparison was no longer possible. After extensive testing, the pilots gave a damning verdict on the WD 8. The flight characteristics in particular were criticised. In spite of its satisfactory climbing ability and speed, the aircraft was very clumsy and not agile enough to take on enemy aircraft. The pilots were therefore even advised to avoid dogfights. The aircraft was also not suitable as a reconnaissance aircraft. Not as a long-range reconnaissance unit because of the limited fuel supply and not as a close-up reconnaissance unit because of the lack of a radio. In addition, the landing speed was too high and the manoeuvrability on the water, especially in waves, left a lot to be desired. Ultimately, the aircraft was judged to be completely unusable and therefore it was requested that the aircraft return to Germany. In the end, the RMA decided to accept the twin-engined solution as a bomber and, in later WD series, also as a torpedo carrier, so the WD 8 remained a one-off.

Gotha WD 9—Armed Sea Reconnaissance Aircraft

As the successor to the single-engined Gotha WD 5, the RMA commissioned GWF on 26 October 1915 to develop an armed version, which was designated Gotha WD 9. It was to be used in the allied Ottoman Navy. Like the WD 5, the two-seater aircraft was powered by a Mercedes D.III with 160 hp. The armament consisted of a machine gun, with which the observer seated behind the pilot could fire forward to a limited extent via an adapted wing. Specifically for the transfer to the Ottoman Empire, a travel axis was built under the floats of the WD 9 so that the aircraft could take off and land from land. The prototype with the Marine number 572 was delivered to the SVK on 19 April 1916. A month later, it was made available to the sea flight station in Zeebrugge for front tests, where it remained until June 1917. There was no series production for the Ottoman Empire, instead the simplified Gotha WD 13 later went into production.

Gotha WD 11—The First Torpedo Aircraft of the Gotha Wagon Factory

After the success with the Gotha WD 7, GWF developed into the preferred contractor for twin-engined floatplanes for the Imperial German Navy. The testing of the WD 7 had just been completed when the RMA commissioned GWF with

The Gotha WD 8 was the single-engined variant of the twin-engined Gotha WD 7. (*Author's collection*)

The armed Gotha WD 9 was a one-off and a further development of the unarmed Gotha WD 5 for the navy of the Ottoman Empire. (*Author's collection*)

the construction of a twin-engined torpedo aircraft that was to serve as a sea scout at the same time. Karl Rösner then developed the WD 7 further into the WD 11. At first glance, both aircraft looked very similar. The WD 11, however, was somewhat larger in size and had more power with two six-cylinder in-line Mercedes D.III engines, each with 160 hp at the pusher propeller. The torpedo hung at a 5-degree incline on a launcher in a recess in the inside of the fuselage. The prototype with the Marine number 679 was taken over by the SVK on 9 October 1916. The development of WD 11 is very well documented on the basis of the SVK's activity reports. In the report of 16 October 1916:

> The acetylene starter built into the Gotha T airplane (torpedo aircraft) Marine number 679 was thoroughly tested. The gas pump with differential piston newly designed by the company was not usable; no start was achieved at all. The reason for this is probably a wrongly chosen mixing ratio. The old pump was then installed, precisely adjusted and tested. Each engine of the aircraft was started ten times without failure. As already reported after previous attempts, the starter is safe and usable if it is correctly set and handled properly.

According to SVK report of 4 November 1916:

> Gotha type aircraft 679 taken over after the problems found were remedied by modification. Damaged in Holtenau when zeroing in the weapons by TVK (Torpedo Test Command), after repairs transferred to Flensburg.

In April 1917, the first three production series of machines of the WD 11 arrived in Warnemünde. In addition to the prototype 679, a total of twelve other Gotha WD 11s with the Marine numbers 991 to 995, 1211 to 1213, and 1372 to 1379 were built in three batches. Starting in May 1917, the II. Torpedo aircraft squadron (*Torpedoversuchskommando*) in Zeebrugge received its first WD 11 and immediately used it against English merchant ships in the North Sea. A formation of three WD 11s attacked the port of Ipswich in England, which was supported by two Friedrichshafen FF 33 Ls, on 14 June 1917. The WD 11, with navy no. 992 and the crew, Leutnant zur See Becker und Vizeflugmeister Mallmann, succeeded in torpedoing and sinking the SS *Kankakee* (a US freighter that had been taken over by the Royal Navy as a transport vessel). Just a month later, 991 and 992 were themselves lost. During an operation against four merchant ships, the 991 was hit by the defensive fire from the freighter and had to make an emergency landing at sea, with the aircraft overturning. The 992 with the Becker/Mallmann crew was able to land next to the 991 and get their two comrades out of the water, but broke down during take-off and was then dependent on help. The two escort aircraft managed to guide a steamer to the scene of the accident, which was able to save the airmen. The aircraft were lost, however, and the four naval aviators fell into British captivity. In the autumn of 1917, nine Gotha WD 11s of the I. Torpedo Airplane Squadron took part in Operation Albion in the Baltic Sea. It was an amphibious

The prototype of the WD 11 with the Marine number 679 on the GWF's water basin, shortly before delivery to the seaplane test command. (*Stiftung Deutsches Technikmuseum Berlin*)

The Gotha WD 11 was able to carry a torpedo that was fastened in a recess under the fuselage. (Gotha City Archives, signature 6.1/1418 Fig. 23)

landing operation of the German army and navy to conquer several strategically important Russian islands off the Riga Bay. Five Gotha WD 11s were supposed to attack two Russian mine-layers off the island of Dagö on 8 October 1917. The attack failed; presumably due to insufficient water depth, three torpedoes went aground and the other two torpedoes also missed the target. This was presumably the last use of German torpedo aircraft during the First World War.

Gotha WD 12—Sea Reconnaissance Aircraft

The Gotha WD 12 is a further development of the WD 9, a single-engined, seaworthy, long-range reconnaissance aircraft that could also drop bombs. Karl Rösner attached particular importance to the light and aerodynamic shape of the fuselage. The propeller had a parabolic cap and merged into a streamlined wooden fuselage. The tubular steel struts of the float frame were also aerodynamically designed with teardrop-shaped plywood cladding. The aircraft had a kerb weight of 1,000 kg. It was powered by a six-cylinder in-line Mercedes D.III engine, which delivered 160 hp. This enabled the WD 12 to reach a top speed of 141 kph. The range was over 700 km. The prototype, with the Marine number 944, was delivered to the SVK in March 1917. During the test, the SVK determined the following flight performance:

> 1,000 m in 7.5 s, 2,000 m in 18 s, 3,000 m in 36 s, it appears that with a performance propeller, the climbing ability could be improved. Sea test on 27 March at a sea state of 4, average start time 13′, turns up to 3 strokes out of the wind when floating, damage to the bottom of the floats and broken fittings in the float frame

Sea scout Gotha WD 12a in 1917 in front of the seaplane test command in Warnemünde. Only this one machine was taken over and used for test purposes. (Rahardt collection)

make reinforcements necessary. The attempts to increase the seaworthiness will be continued after the reconstruction by the company at SVK.[5]

The improved prototype, then designated Gotha WD 12 a, was tested again by the SVK:

After the reconstruction on 8 May passed the sea test very well. The water landing was very smooth despite the relatively high landing speed. Drifting and rolling through the wind were also achieved without problems. The type would be recommended to the RMA for re-ordering with minor changes, the aircraft (the prototype) is temporarily being withheld in Warnemünde for test purposes.[6]

But the RMA did not request any more WD 12. Instead, the Ottoman Empire ordered the aircraft, six with a Mercedes D.III and three with a Benz Bz.III engine.

Gotha WD 13—Sea Reconnaissance Aircraft, Training Aircraft, 'Turkish Aircraft'

The Gotha WD 13 was an armed, single-engined training aircraft with dual controls designed by Karl Rösner for the Turkish Navy. The two-seater biplane was a simplified version of the Gotha WD 9, to which it looked very similar. Compared to the WD 9, which was equipped with a 160-hp Mercedes D.III, the WD 13 received the somewhat weaker Benz Bz.III with 150 hp. A machine gun was installed in the rear observer stand to defend against enemy aircraft. Six Gotha WD 13s were built at the end of 1917/beginning of 1918 and delivered to the Ottoman Empire after acceptance by the SVK.

At the end of 1917, on behalf of the Ottoman Navy, the GWF designed the Gotha WD 13, an armed training aircraft with dual controls. Here photographed in front of the SVK in Warnemünde. (*Author's collection*)

Gotha WD 14—Torpedo Bomber, Long-Range Reconnaissance Aircraft

After the Benz company had developed a new 220-hp six-cylinder in-line engine with the Benz IV at the beginning of 1916, the RMA commissioned GWF in June 1916 to design a twin-engined torpedo aircraft with this new motor. Based on the predecessor, model WD 11, Karl Rösner developed the Gotha WD 14. Similar in concept, the WD 14 made quite a few changes compared to its predecessor, which had been equipped with a pusher propeller. The two Benz Bz.IVs with 200 hp each, which were mounted on the lower wing to the right and left of the fuselage, were designed with a tractor propeller. In the widened fuselage, the pilot and observer sat side by side. The aircraft had a dual rudder so that the two crewmembers could relieve each other on longer flights. To save space in a hangar or on board a ship, the wings could be folded alongside the fuselage. As with the WD 11, a torpedo or mines could be carried in a recess under the fuselage. As a defensive armament, the aircraft was equipped with machine guns pointing forwards and backwards. The first Gotha WD 14 with the navy no. 801 was delivered to Warnemünde in January 1917. The first tests took place in early February 1917. The SVK inspectors criticised the inadequate effect of the rudder and ordered larger control surfaces from GWF. The positive performance of the improved machine, then designated as WD 14a, led to a follow-up order from the RMA for 16 torpedo bombers (Marine numbers 1415 to 1430) one month later. The order was adjusted even before series production began. The GWF was to build only six torpedo planes from this series and deliver the other ten as long-range reconnaissance aircraft. The remaining ten machines were to be equipped with an additional tank and radio equipment. The reason for the conversion of the order was a blatant shortage of torpedoes, which were primarily made available for the submarines. The first WD 14 was built as a long-range reconnaissance aircraft with navy no. 1415 and was delivered by GWF to the SVK on 11 July 1917. During this time, aircraft of this size were now referred to as large aircraft (*Großflugzeuge*) in the navy, as has long been the norm in the army. The third series ordered by the RMA also consisted of twelve long-range reconnaissance aircraft (Marine numbers 1617 to 1628) and torpedo planes (Marine numbers 1651 to 1662) and were delivered from November 1917. Another 25 WD 14s (marine numbers 1946 to 1970) were ordered by the RMA in October 1917. A total of 66 Gotha WD 14s were built, but they were no longer used as torpedo bombers; instead, they were mainly put to use as long-range reconnaissance vehicles, and as bombers. After the only modest successes of the German torpedo pilots, which were associated with a high level of personnel and technical effort, the navy disbanded the two torpedo aircraft squadrons at the end of 1917. The new task of the large aircraft was the reconnaissance of British ship movements in the North Sea. In this role they replaced the navy's cumbersome airships. The action radius of up to 8½ hours also contributed to this. However, tough operating conditions over the North Sea, engine malfunctions, and poor seaworthiness also made things difficult for the crews. There were repeated ditchings, which in the worst case led to total loss. Nevertheless, the WD 14s were

The first Gotha WD 14, Marine number 801. The GWF delivered it to the SVK in January 1917. Although designed as a torpedo bomber, the Gotha WD 14 was mainly used as a long-range reconnaissance aircraft. (*Author's collection*)

To save space, the WD 14 was equipped with folding wings. (*Gotha City Archives, signature 6.1/1418 image 25*)

relatively successful under the adverse circumstances. Building on this experience, the *Reichs-Marine-Amt* then commissioned further developments in Gotha specifically designed as long-range reconnaissance aircraft.

Gotha WD 15—Sea Reconnaissance

The two-seater Gotha WD 15 was a seaworthy, unarmed reconnaissance aircraft and at the same time, the last single-engined aircraft of the WD series to be built in series by GWF. It was basically a slightly enlarged WD 12, from which it took over the aerodynamic shape and the wooden construction. The aircraft was powered by a six-cylinder in-line Mercedes D.IVa engine with 260 hp. The top speed was 152 kph and the range was 900 km. This allowed reconnaissance flights of up to six hours. At the beginning of June 1917, the first prototype with Marine number 842 was tested at SVK Warnemünde. During the test flights, the SVK pilots repeatedly had to struggle with engine problems that constantly interrupted the flight programme. As stated in the SVK report on the WD 15 from 7 September:

> Still in flight testing, the testing was delayed again by another engine breakdown. After the experiences made here where three Mercedes engines have been built into the aircraft one after the other, it seems doubtful that the engine in its current version can be used for long overseas flights.[7]

When the engine ran, the testers certified that the WD 15 had good overall flight characteristics. At the beginning of September, the 842 was destroyed in a float breakage. The SVK then ordered a new WD 15, which was equipped with reinforced floats. On 17 October 1917, the aircraft with the marine no. 843 was delivered to Warnemünde. However, the engine breakdowns continued, so the test programme had to be interrupted again. There was no series production of the WD 15, and the RMA of GWF transferred the licence production of the single-engined reconnaissance aircraft to Friedrichshafen FF 49c in July 1918.

Gotha WD 20—Torpedo Bomber, Long-Range Reconnaissance Aircraft

The Gotha WD 20 was built in mid-1917 after an RMA tender for a seaworthy, long-range reconnaissance aircraft. In principle, Rösner developed the WD 14 further into the WD 20. The dimensions of the two aircraft were roughly identical. Two machine guns were installed as defensive armament, which could fire forwards and backwards. The aircraft was powered by two six-cylinder in-line Mercedes D.IVa engines with 260 hp each. In the recess on the inside of the fuselage, an additional drop-tank or a torpedo could be installed. This meant that the machine could also be used as a torpedo bomber, and to increase the range, 20 additional fuel tanks were installed in the fuselage. The associated higher weight

Gotha WD 15, Marine number 843 on the water basin in Gotha, shortly before delivery to the SVK. (*Author's collection*)

The Gotha WD 20 long-range reconnaissance aircraft shortly before delivery to the Navy in May 1918. The folding wings were now installed as standard. (*Stiftung Deutsches Technikmuseum Berlin*)

called for larger floats, but this meant that the aircraft was relatively heavy. On 2 May 1918, the GWF delivered the first WD 20 with the Marine number 1515 to the SVK. During testing, the SVK determined there to be a 'strong aft load'. The two rear tanks, the machine guns, and the radio were then removed one after the other. However, even a stronger sweep of the wings could not completely solve the problem. With these severe restrictions, shorter range, no machine guns, and radio equipment, combined with poor flight characteristics, the SVK classified the Gotha WD 20 as no longer suitable for the front. The aircraft was only suitable for torpedo training purposes.[8] Two more WD 20s (Marine numbers 1516 and 1517) were built in Gotha and delivered to the SVK on 27 May and 27 June 1918.

Gotha WD 22—Long-Range Reconnaissance Aircraft, Experimental Aircraft

On 9 October 1917, the RMA ordered two Gotha WD 22 from GWF. Based on the experience with the WD 20, chief designer Karl Rösner designed a four-engined biplane with floats and a wingspan of 26 metres. To the right and left of the fuselage, two engines were installed in tandem in two engine pods between the wings. In front, a 160-hp Mercedes D.III with a tractor propeller and behind it a Mercedes D.I with 100 hp which drove a pusher propeller. With a total of 260 hp per nacelle, the same engine power was installed as in the WD 20 with just one engine. The first WD 22 was given the Marine number 2133 and was handed over to the SVK for testing in May 1918. As with the WD 20, the WD 22 also turned out to be too tail-heavy. The GWF then changed the sweep of the wings. The second WD 22 was delivered with the Marine number 2134. GWF delivered 2134 on 21 August 1918. This aircraft differed from 2133 by the reversed engine arrangement in the nacelles. The weaker Mercedes engine was in front, behind it

Long-range reconnaissance aircraft Gotha WD 22, Marine number 2133. The WD 22 was basically a WD 20 converted to four engines. (*Stiftung Deutsches Technikmuseum Berlin*)

the more powerful Mercedes engine. The two aircraft were seaworthy and also airworthy, even with only three engines. As with the land-based Gotha bombers G IV and G V, the WD 22 had a firing channel in the rear machine-gun defence post, the 'Gotha tunnel' for defence downwards. In a recess on the underside, the aircraft could carry either an additional tank, a torpedo, or bombs.

Gotha WD 27—Long-Range Reconnaissance Aircraft

The Gotha WD 27 long-range reconnaissance aircraft, designed by Karl Rösner, was the conclusion and highlight of Gotha's seaplane production. With a wingspan of 34 metres, it was the largest aircraft ever built in Gotha. The WD 27 was created at the end of 1918 when the RMA requested a long-range reconnaissance aircraft with floats for long-distance reconnaissance flights over the sea. Building on the experience gained from the WD 22, Rösner adopted the concept with two coupled motors, which were each mounted in tandem in nacelles between the wings. Four super-compressed Mercedes D.IIIas with 175 hp each were installed. In terms of construction, the Gotha WD 27 was a four-bay biplane with a wooden fuselage that tapered towards the end of the fuselage. As with the previous models, the WD 27 had foldable, wooden wings, which enabled the span to be reduced from 34 metres to 10.5 metres. The dual elevator and vertical stabiliser system was a pure tubular steel construction similar to that found on a biplane. The two pilots sat next to each other. The aircraft had a dual rudder so that either pilot could take over control of the aircraft. The cabin for the radio operator and the rear defence post with a machine gun were located behind the pilot's cabin. A forward-facing machine gun was installed in a second defensive position in front of the pilot's cabin. Both defences were easily accessible from the inside via the pilot's cabin. In addition to the fuel tank built into the fuselage, a second tank was attached underneath, which could be thrown off in an emergency. These two containers had a total capacity of 1,790 litres and thus enabled reconnaissance flights of up to eight hours. The top speed was 141 kph, or 105 kph if an engine failed. The RMA commissioned three of these aircraft with the Marine numbers 4326, 4327, and 4328 from GWF in mid-1918. Probably the only WD 27 that was completed was Marine number 4326, which only left the GWF assembly hall in January 1919, after the end of the war. Plans to convert the WD 27 into a cargo or passenger aircraft failed due to the veto of the Allies, who decided to scrap the machine.

Gotha WD 28—Sea Reconnaissance

With the Gotha WD 28, GWF received the order for a single-engined reconnaissance aircraft with radio equipment in July 1918. The six-cylinder in-line Mercedes D.IVa engine with 260 hp was planned. At Daimler, the motor replaced the

The four-engined long-distance reconnaissance aircraft Gotha WD 27 under construction. As with the previous models, the folding wings were standard. (*Author's collection*)

Group picture: *from the right*: engineer Albrecht Klaube, designer Karl Rösner, Director-General Albert Kandt, Major Blattmann, operations manager Rhein, and operations assistant Wagner. Behind them is the four-engined Gotha WD 27 designed by Rösner, the largest aircraft ever built by GWF with a wingspan of 34 metres. To the left of it is a twin-engined Gotha GL X high-altitude reconnaissance aircraft. Neither aircraft were used in the war. (*Author's collection*)

eight-cylinder in-line engine Mercedes D.IV with 220 hp, which had also powered the actually quite promising Gotha WD 15 but caused constant malfunctions in this aircraft. The RMA ordered a total of four machines in Gotha, three with radio equipment (Marine numbers 4001 to 4003) and one (Marine number 4034) that could carry bombs. The first two prototypes of the draft made by Rösner are said to have been under construction when all work had to be stopped in early 1919.

Friedrichshafen FF 49c—Sea Reconnaissance Aircraft (Licence Built)

On 30 July 1918, GWF received an order from the RMA to produce 30 units of the Friedrichshafen FF49c under licence. The aircraft was a single-engined biplane, armed with two machine guns, powered by a 240-hp Benz Bz.V. The machines from Gotha production were to be given Marine numbers 4004 to 4033. Only one FF 49c is said to have been built in Gotha by the end of the war.

6

1919–1933:
Suspension of Aircraft Construction

In addition to wagon construction and aircraft construction, GWF's corporate headquarters planned the development of a third business area at the beginning of 1916—locomotive construction. In connection with this, the aircraft construction department was to be relocated from Gotha to Fürth in Bayern.[9] GWF had bought land here and founded a subsidiary, *Bayerischen Waggon- und Flugzeugwerke gegründet*. Due to the high-capacity utilisation at the end of 1916, however, relocating aircraft construction to Fürth would have resulted in a loss of production, so the move was postponed until after the war. With the Armistice on 11 November 1918 and the peace conditions imposed on the German Reich in the Treaty of Versailles, these plans never came to fruition. Due to a provision in the Treaty of Versailles, aircraft construction in Gotha had to be completely stopped and all existing production facilities and drawings destroyed. In addition, the Gotha airship hangar and the facilities of the FEA 3 had to be demolished—everything was carried out under the control of the Inter-Allied Military Monitoring Commission, which meticulously monitored the implementation of these provisions. At the end of 1918, GWF had a total of 2,000 employees, 1,300 of whom were employed in aircraft construction alone. All of them were suddenly out of work. Not only the workers, but the two chief designers were also forced to leave Gotha.

Crisis Years—The Economic Development of the Gotha Wagon Factory up to 1933

It was a very difficult time for GWF. With the end of aircraft construction and the generally very difficult economic situation in post-war Germany, the company was on the verge of collapse several times. Since aircraft construction no longer

Only scrap: According to the provisions in the Treaty of Versailles, all aircraft parts, tools, and construction plans of the aircraft construction department had to be destroyed after the war. (*Author's collection*)

seemed possible in the near future, GWF leased small parts of its airfield to its own workers for agricultural use. They were not only forced to think once more about the construction and repair of passenger and freight cars, but also to open up completely new fields of production. For a while, they kept afloat with the construction of furniture, winter sports equipment, and truck trailers. The entry into locomotive construction, which had already been planned during the war, was discontinued in 1924 after the manufacture of some replacement boilers. After that, the construction of trams developed very successfully. In 1921, GWF ventured into the automotive industry and took over the Eisenacher vehicle factory. At that time, Eisenach mainly built British Morris cars for the German market and was initially very successful. In 1926, GWF Director-General Albert Kandt died unexpectedly during a business trip. In the same year, GWF merged with Cyklon Automobilwerke AG with branches in Berlin and Mylau in Saxony; however, this merger did not bring GWF into the black numbers it had hoped for. On the contrary, the company slid even deeper into the crisis. The catastrophic economic situation became public knowledge. GWF, with its three branches in Gotha, Eisenach, and Fürth, was heavily in debt. The main reason for the imbalance was the poor order situation of wagon construction. In addition, there was a lack of profitability in production. A bank consortium, now majority shareholder of the company, took over the helm and pursued a tough restructuring exercise, which was primarily at the expense of the employees. Kurt Toltz, successor to Albert Kandt as managing director of GWF, got involved in politics and was also head of the local council building/planning department, which in turn was supposed to put pressure on the state-owned German *Reichsbahngesellschaft* (predecessor to the German Railway) to place new orders with the GWF.[10] That actually succeeded, but GWF was by no means restructured. Therefore, the focus was on the core business, and in 1928, the deficit-running automobile construction plant was sold again. In addition to the two former Cyklon factories in Mylau and Berlin, GWF also parted ways with the automobile plant in Eisenach. On 14 November 1928, the *Bayerische Motorenwerke* (BMW) bought the plant—and with this purchase, they entered the automotive industry for the first time. This heralded the complete end of the Kandt era in the GWF: Albert Kandt's son, Albert Kandt Jr, remained at BMW, where he would rise from test driver and employee to commercial director of BMW Eisenach by 1945. BMW, whose automobiles were exclusively produced in Eisenach until 1945, now benefited from the new vehicle developments initiated during the GWF period. With the sale of the automotive division, GWF was still unable to really get ahead due to the core business, wagon construction, still being

In 1921, GWF entered the automotive industry with the takeover of the Eisenacher vehicle factory. Commencing in 1928 the Dixi 3/15 was built in Eisenach, a licence from the British Austin Seven. After the takeover by BMW, it became the BMW 3/15. (*Author's collection*)

underutilised. There was still a lack of orders from the Reichsbahn (German railway), so old connections were considered. Through the mediation of the former ducal family of Sachsen-Coburg und Gotha, who were also related to the Bulgarian tsar, it was possible to get orders from the Bulgarian railway company. However, that too was only a brief revival of wagon construction in Gotha, which was still in deep crisis throughout Germany. Many German wagon construction companies merged or were taken over during this time. That is what happened to GWF. In April 1930, the Berlin mechanical engineering group Orenstein & Koppel took over 90 per cent of the share capital of Gothaer Waggonfabrik from the Schapiro Group (Jakob Schapiro was a well-known stock market speculator at the time), which owned GWF after the restructuring. The new parent company gradually nurtured GWF again and, among other things, provided employment by relocating the production of diesel railcars to Gotha. The wagon construction remained a problem child, even as things slowly started to improve. While GWF only had 205 employees in its two locations of Gotha and Fürth on 1 April 1932, exactly one year later, it was 259, and at the end of 1933, 563. This increase in employment is explained by the takeover of power by the National Socialists in Germany, starting on 30 January 1933. That marked the beginning of a new chapter in the history of the Gotha wagon factory.

7

1933–1945: Gotha Wagon Factory Produces Aircraft Again

Immediately after the NSDAP (*Nationalsozialistische Deutsche Arbeiterpartei* or 'Nazis') came to power, the initially covert and then, from 1935 on, open rearmament of the German military began. This also included a powerful air force, from which Germany had been banned by the Treaty of Versailles. On 2 February 1933, just three days after taking power, the new Reich government set up the first new structures for future aviation in Germany. On this day, the *Reichskommissariat für Luftfahrt* (Reich Commissariat for Aviation—RKL) was founded, which took over the tasks of the aviation department of the Reich Ministry of Transport with retroactive effect from 30 January 1933, which until then had been headed by the former commander of the Bogohl 3, Ernst Brandenburg, who was immediately released from his duties. *Reichsluftfahrtministerium* (The Reich Aviation Ministry—RLM) emerged from the RKL under the leadership of Hermann Göring in April 1933. Göring was a veteran First World War fighter pilot ace, he was a recipient of the *Pour le Mérite* ('The Blue Max'). He had been the last commander of *Jagdgeschwader* 1 (*Jasta* 1), the fighter wing once led by Manfred von Richthofen.

State Secretary Erhard Milch was responsible for building up the air force and at the same time the most powerful man behind Göring. According to the motto 'everything that flies is subject to the RLM', the ministry immediately brought all civil aviation structures under state control. The local associations organised in the German Aviation Association were dissolved and liquidated. Its more than 60,000 members were able to join the *Deutschen Luftsportverband* (German Air Sports Association—DLV) and thus became a uniform entity. The work of the DLV was based on purely military aspects and structures. The RLM became the sole client for the German aviation industry. The ministry not only determined which aircraft were built, but also which manufacturer had to build aircraft under licence or which types were to be approved for export. The companies were divided into different categories. There were the established manufacturers such as Heinkel, Arado, or Junkers who received development contracts from the RLM to build new aircraft. There were also licensing companies, to which the GWF, Erla, or AGO later belonged, and the repair shops. The German aviation industry could count on generous and cheap government support in the form of loans and equity investments when expanding its production capacities. It was, in fact, nationalisation through the back door. The need for all kinds of aircraft at this time was huge, and even companies that up to this point had not been involved in the industry could sense big business. Since rail vehicle construction was still very unsatisfactory at the time, the Gothaer Waggonfabrik also decided to return to aircraft construction. Although aircraft from Gotha had a certain degree of popularity due to their missions in the First World War, the resumption of aircraft construction from the end of 1933 onwards was equivalent to a new beginning. After all, there were neither factory buildings nor an airfield (now used as a field). There were also no specialist staff remaining in Gotha. In the absence of their own product, the Gothaer initially wanted to start manufacturing under license.[11] After positive discussions with the RLM about the possibility of taking over a licence model, the GWF contacted the aircraft manufacturers Junkers and Heinkel via the technical office LC in the RLM. Junkers was busy and cancelled. Heinkel, on the other hand, was more accessible and offered GWF the prospect of licensing the Heinkel He 72 sports aircraft for 22,000 Reichsmarks.[12] For unknown reasons, there was no contract and no production. At the same time, GWF managing director Kurt Toltz tried to bring a designer to Gotha in order to be able to design and build his own aircraft again at some point. On 15 November 1933, Toltz informed the lord mayor of Gotha, Dr Fritz Schmidt, that 'The Gotha Wagon Factory has employed a skilled engineer to design an aircraft.'[13] The new designer was Albert Kalkert (1902–1977), whom Toltz and his employees were able to recruit from the engineering school in Weimar to take on the new Department of Aircraft Construction and work in Gotha. Good pay and an attractive environment certainly played a role for Kalkert, but there was also the risk of failure if the GWF Technical Office did not assign development contracts. From Weimar, Kalkert brought the design of a heavy, single-engined training biplane with him—the later-named Gotha Go 145. Until new offices were built on the GWF factory premises, the development team first met in Kalkert's private apartment. Except for the engine, the mock-up of the biplane was ready on 19 December 1933. The prototype flew for the first time in early 1934. The GWF then presented the aircraft, which was developed without an order and at its own risk, to the RLM. The plan worked, because the Technical Office had an interest in having another B-1 class training aircraft produced alongside the Arado Ar 66, which was already in production. GWF boss Kurt Toltz had achieved a great coup. Although only classified as a licensed manufacturer, GWF was now able to produce its own sample in series. Also, in addition to Erla and AGO, established German manufacturers such as Bayerische Flugzeugwerke and Focke Wulf later had to build the Gotha 145. The biplane was even an export success. In addition to deliveries to Austria, Romania, and Turkey, the model was manufactured under licence in Spain. However, the licence production of the Heinkel He 45 and He 46 had top priority. Series production of the Go 145 only began in 1936, two years after the first flight.

A new start: With the training biplane Gotha Go 145, GWF succeeded in creating its first successful in-house design. (*DEHLA*)

A press photograph: Go 145 (in flight) in front of the Gotha Go 146 touring aircraft, the first Gotha aircraft with retractable landing gear, which took off for the first time on 14 December 1936. (*Author's collection*)

Restructuring and Licensed Construction

With the prospect of large-scale production of aircraft, substantial investments were made into expanding the plant in Gotha. In addition to the reactivated airfield, which was put back into operation from 1934 and expanded in the following years, production halls, a training workshop, and an administrative building were built. In addition to expanding the production area in Gotha, GWF founded a branch in Ilmenau, 40 km away, in September 1936. Gotha-Ilmenauer Flugzeugbau GmbH, as its own supplier, was primarily supposed to produce semi-finished products—for example, raw material components made of wood for the construction of wings. The parts were then transported by rail to Gotha for final assembly, and the Ilmenau branch was given its own rail connection especially for this purpose. GWF boss Kurt Toltz and Albert Kalkert took over the management in Ilmenau as deputies. Series production of the Go 145 did not begin until the beginning of 1936. First, GWF had to build under licence. The first planes were the two short-range reconnaissance aircraft Heinkel He 45 and He 46, later the Focke-Wulf Fw 58 training aircraft and the DFS 230 cargo glider. These aircraft were built in a classic composite construction with a covered tubular steel fuselage, wooden wings, and tail unit. The Messerschmitt Bf 110, a completely metal construction, would also be manufactured under licence. In 1938, after a long search for investors, the GWF parted with its subsidiary, the Bavarian wagon and aircraft works in Fürth. The operating portion went to the Bachmann company, von Blumenthal & Co. KG in Fürth, a repair shop for aircraft.

The administration building built in the 1930s as it stands today. (*Author's collection*)

A glance into the design office of GWF. (*Schinnerling collection*)

GWF works meeting: *first row, fourth from left*, chief designer Albert Kalkert. In the background: open loading ramps of the Go 242 cargo gliders. The photograph was taken on the air base around 1940, after the combat squadron had left for war. The assembly of the gliders was relocated to the empty halls. (*Schinnerling collection*)

Personnel Upheaval in 1940–41

Shortly after the start of the war, GWF's own designs were no longer in demand. The last self-developed planes were the cargo glider Go 242 and the motorised version Go 244. Although these two aircraft were put into production, the Technical Office no longer gave GWF new development contracts. It was therefore foreseeable that the future lay solely in the business of licence construction. Resignations commenced; many leading employees, some of whom had come to Gotha from the engineering school in Weimar with Kalkert, left GWF in quick succession. Kalkert also left in October 1940, after clearly having problems with GWF boss Kurt Toltz. He moved to Erfurt, 25 km away, where he managed the Erfurt Repair Plant (REWE), which later became the Central German Metal Works. There was also a change in personnel in the executive suite of the Gotha Wagon Factory. Kurt Toltz, who had led the GWF through the crisis since 1926 after the sudden death of Albert Kandt, and who had returned the company to aircraft manufacturing, retired in 1941. The new managing directors of GWF and the subsidiary in Ilmenau came from the parent company Ohrenstein & Koppel (changed in 1942 to Maschinenbau und Bahn AG). The new directors were the lawyer Georg Haller from Berlin and Dr Karl Peter Berthold and Dr Gustav Dietz from Gotha. Kalkert's successor with regard to the operational process was Albert Hünerjäger. In the meantime, the war had also made itself felt in the composition of the GWF workforce. In 1942 alone, 1,078 workers had to join the *Wehrmacht*

Orientated towards war: GWF works meeting in front of a Führer portrait and Bf 110. The photo was taken around 1943. (*Dlugosch collection*)

(German army). The gaps were filled by women, who between 1941 and the end of 1942 rose from 12.2 per cent to 25 per cent of the total workforce. There were also around 2,000 forced labourers and 100 Soviet prisoners of war. That was one quarter of the 8,165 GWF employees.[14] The focus of production at this time was on the initial production series of the Go 242 and the Messerschmitt Bf 110. This aircraft was taken out of the Messerschmitt AG production in 1941. With these changes, the GWF was not only one of the two main producers of the Bf 110, the other being the Luther works in Braunschweig, but was also responsible for the further development of the heavy fighter, which was now mainly produced as a night pursuit aircraft.

Bombing Raids and Relocation of Production

As an armaments company important to the war effort, GWF quickly caught the attention of the Allies. However, it was not until 1944 that the company was included in the target planning. The Allies described a series of bombing raids as 'Big Week', aimed at destroying the German aviation industry; on 24 February 1944, 239 B-24 Liberators of the 8th USAAF approached the Gothaer Waggonfabrik. In the face of heavy resistance from German fighters, 169 bombers reached Gotha and dropped a total of 372 tons of bombs over the GWF premises. The bombing caused severe damage to the plant, especially in the area of aircraft construction. With the exception of the administration building, all production halls were more or less destroyed. Many roofs even collapsed. However, under the rubble, the machine tools remained relatively undamaged, so they were able to start production again without losing much time. Numerous Bf 110s that were on the airfield were destroyed or severely damaged. A total of 232 workers were killed. The production hiatus lasted six to seven weeks, which meant that 140 Bf 110s could not be produced. As further attacks were to be expected, GWF began to relocate production to 24 branch offices within Gotha and the surrounding areas. For example, the airframes were assembled in Goldbach. The relocated machine tools of GWF were stored in the railway tunnel between Reinhardsbrunn and Friedrichroda. The experimental building moved into the Ortlepp Joinery in Friedrichroda. Other departments were moved to Wangenheim, Luisenthal, Gräfentonna, Wandersleben, and Ohrdruf, among others. Another attack followed on 20 July 1944, again by the 8th USAAF. The damage in the area of aircraft construction was minor this time due to the relocation of production, but it hit the wagon construction area with full force. Not only railway wagons were being built there, but also semi-truck trailers were built for the road transport of tanks and guns.

1933–1945: Gotha Wagon Factory Produces Aircraft Again

The American air raid on 24 February 1944 caused severe damage to the production facilities. (*Gotha City Archives, signature 5.1/2580 image 144*)

In the same attack, the night fighter Bf 110 G-4 was destroyed. (*Gotha City Archives, signature 5.1/2580 image 184*)

Materials Shortage and Production Cessation

At the end of 1944 and the beginning of 1945, the shortage of materials led to severe production restrictions at GWF. The Allied bombing raids on the German rail system, the armaments industry, and their suppliers showed their effectiveness. There were frequent production stoppages, and in 1945 only a few Bf 110s could be delivered. In fact, production was supposed to be phased out in December 1944 in favour of the Focke Wulf Ta 152. The plan was to assemble two Ta 152s a month starting in February 1945. By July 1945, production was even to be increased to 70 units a month, but this plan failed, as did the production of the flying wing Horten Ho 229. GWF leadership therefore placed high hopes on the Gotha P-60 flying wing jet fighter designed as an alternative to the Ho 229. With this design, GWF could have put out its first self-designed aircraft since the Go 242/244. At the beginning of April 1945, shortly before the American invasion, production collapsed completely. On 4 April 1945, the Gotha Wagon Factory was occupied by US troops.

8

Aircraft 1933–1945

Gotha Go 145—Training Aircraft

The two-seater Gotha Go 145 training aircraft was a braced, single-bay biplane with a composite construction. In the covered tubular steel fuselage, there were two seats with dual controls, one behind the other. The two-spar wings, rounded at the ends, were made of wood. A special design feature of the biplane was the arrow-shaped upper wing and the straight lower wing. The aileron was made of light metal and covered with fabric. An air-cooled eight-cylinder in-line Argus As 10c engine with 240 hp served as the power plant. The first flight took place in early 1934, the pilot being the former DVS flight instructor Walter Fremd. Two years later, after the Go 145 was included in the delivery programme of the RLM, series production began in Gotha and shortly afterwards also under licence at Erla, AGO, Focke-Wulf, and the Bayerische Flugzeugwerke. The model was also well received abroad; the Go 145 was exported to Austria, Romania, and Turkey. Slovakia received some machines from Luftwaffe stocks. These aircraft were used by Czechoslovakia along with other abandoned aircraft after the Second World War. Spain also acquired a licence and the aircraft built there were given the designation CASA 1145-L. The RLM, which received 50 per cent of the income from the licence fee, also benefited from the export.[15] In addition to the unarmed Gotha Go 145 A, GWF also developed the Go 145 B version as a touring aircraft with a closed canopy and covered landing gear based on the basic model. The Go 145 C was a training aircraft with an MG 15 in a rear defence stand (a 7.92-mm machine gun designed specifically as a hand-manipulated defensive gun for combat aircraft during the early 1930s). The aircraft was specially developed by GWF for the training of gunmen. The Go 145 D had a closed canopy, a covered landing gear, and had bomb locks under the wings. All of these variants remained unique, none of them were produced in series. In April 1941, a Go 145 was used

A number of brand-new Gotha Go 145 As, at the end of the 1930s at the GWF works. (*DEHLA*)

Gotha Go 145 A delivered to Turkey. The aircraft were transferred by air. The Turks had already bought GWF aircraft 20 years earlier. (*DEHLA*)

The Gotha Go 145 C with a MG 15 in the rear defence post did not go into production. (*Author's collection*)

as a test vehicle for the Argus As 014 pulsejet engine (designated 109-014 by the RLM), the later engine of the V1 flying bomb (Fi 103). The Go 145 (D-IIWS) with the 465-hp Argus As 410A-1 engine was used for the test series. At the end of the war, the training biplane also had to go to the front. The fact that the Argus As 10c in the Go 145 only used normal aviation fuel played a decisive role. Aviation fuel was still available in sufficient quantities, while the higher octane fuel required for the Bf 109 or Fw 190 fighter planes was scarcely available. Combined in so-called disruptive combat groups, the Go 145 bombed enemy troop gatherings at night, following the Soviet model. Of the 1,182 Go 145s built between 1936 and 1940, of which 584 were built in Gotha, only one survived the war. The wreck, of which nothing more than the fuselage frame is left, is owned by the Saxon Association for Historical Aircraft e.V. in Dresden and is to be restored as the only specimen preserved worldwide.

Albert Kalkert

Albert Kalkert was born in 1902 in Honigsessen near Siegen. After leaving high school in Neuss in 1918, his ambition was to join the air force, but with the end of the war, this was not possible. However, the idea of flying never let go of him, and while studying engineering at the Polytechnic in Friedberg in 1921, he and other students built their first glider that he flew from the Wasserkuppe in the Rhön. It was there that Kalkert also met Oskar Ursinus who was employed as a designer at Heinkel in 1925. Two years later, he moved to Raab-Katzenstein in

Kassel, which successfully supplied the sports aircraft market with their aircraft. In 1927, he moved to Dornier in Friedrichshafen, where he stayed for five years. In his spare time, Kalkert designed several of his own aircraft. For example, the high-wing KE-5 'Butterfly', the four-seater KE-14 touring aircraft, and the KE-8 light aircraft. These constructions, which were almost all built by the aircraft construction company Ramor in Graz, were characterised by their consistent lightweight construction. In 1933, Kalkert accepted a teaching position in aircraft construction at the engineering school in Weimar, before being lured away by Kurt Toltz as chief designer for the Gothaer wagon factory in the same year. In October 1940, he left Gotha and became director of the Erfurt Repair Plant (REWE). Initially, he engaged in the repair of Luftwaffe aircraft. Later, aircraft such as the Focke-Wulf types Fw 190, Ta 154, and Ta 152 were assembled there. In 1943, in Erfurt, Kalkert designed a successor to the Go 242, the Kalkert Ka 430, which flew for the first time on 27 March 1944. The cargo glider was designed for 12 paratroopers or cargo. With this aircraft, he outdid his former employer, GWF, which was unsuccessful with its designs for a successor to the Go 242. After the war, Kalkert left Erfurt and never found his way back to aircraft construction. In 1953, he became the technical director of the wagon factory Gebrüder Credé in Kassel, a manufacturer of trams and passenger cars. In 1957, he moved to BMW AG in Munich. Three years later, Kalkert became the managing director of Ruhrstahl AG in Witten, where he stayed until his retirement in 1967. Albert Kalkert died in 1977.

Albert Kalkert (*centre*) framed by Hugo Harmens (*left*) and Walter Wundes (*right*), the head of production at GWF. Behind them is a Go 150. (*DEHLA*)

Gotha Go 146—Touring Aircraft

In August 1935, the technical office of the RLM issued a development contract for a high-speed touring aircraft that was to be powered by two Hirth HM 508B. The order went to the company Klemm in Böblingen and GWF. With the assigned RLM version number 146, the design team led by Albert Kalkert proved that a modern monoplane with retractable landing gear could also be built in Gotha. The fuselage of the cantilevered low-wing aircraft with gull wing was designed in all-metal shell construction with an oval cross-section. The wing centre section, in which the tanks were located, the ailerons, and the landing flaps were also made of light metal. The outer wings and the tail unit were made of wood. The hydraulic retractable landing gear was located in the two nacelles. Although the RLM complained that the fuselage was too narrow when inspecting the dummy, the first and second prototypes were built according to this design. On 14 December 1936, the Go 146 V1 took off for its maiden flight with GWF chief pilot Hugo Harmens (1910–2000) at the controls. The second prototype, the Go 146 V2, D-ILPC flew for the first time in early 1937. The two test models were each powered by two Argus As 10C engines. It was not until the third machine, the Go 146 V3, D-ICDY, that the intended Hirth HM 508B engine was used. Compared to the V1 and V2, this prototype also had a widened fuselage to create additional space for a fourth passenger. But it was already too late. The competition for the touring aircraft had meanwhile been won by the Siebel Fh 104 model. In addition to the three prototypes, a small production series of four Go 146s was created, which were used as liaison aircraft.

Gotha Go 147—Experimental Aircraft

In October 1934, the technical office of the RLM commissioned GWF and the German Research Institute for Glider Flight (DFS) with the construction of a tailless test aircraft. Specifically, the order went to two pioneers in this field, the aircraft designer Alexander Lippisch (1894–1976) for DFS, and to the physicist and aerodynamicist Dr August Kupper (1905–1937), who was supposed to implement his design at GWF. Both had already gained experience in building tailless gliders. In connection with the lower construction costs and lower air resistance, the RLM was looking for a military version as a close-up reconnaissance aircraft. Since tailless aircraft are constructed without a detached horizontal stabilizer, they have a clear view and thus a wide field of fire to the rear. Dr Kupper's design was called the Gotha Go 147 and was an arrow-shaped, high-wing aircraft with wooden wings in a V-shape, wing end plates as vertical tail and combined ailerons and elevators on the edges of the outer wings. The fuselage with the engine in front consisted of a tubular steel frame partially covered with sheet metal and covered with fabric. Pilot and observer sat in two open seats, one behind the other, in the rear of the fuselage. In June 1935, GWF presented the mock-up of their Go 147,

The Go 146 touring aircraft was the first Gotha aircraft to have an all-metal shell construction and retractable landing gear. (*DEHLA*)

Gotha Go 146 exhibited at the International Aviation Salon in Brussels in July 1939. (*DEHLA*)

equipped with a Siemens rotary engine. It was clear to Kupper that the properties of his test aircraft had to be measured against those of a conventional model. He expected to have to repeatedly adapt the aircraft technically and aerodynamically after the tests. Difficulties in steering around the vertical axis were to be expected, especially during take-off and landing. For the tests, the Go 147 received a main landing gear that could be moved forwards and backwards with a steerable and brake-able tail wheel. This enabled the optimal centre of gravity to be found.[16] The first prototype, the Go 147 V1, then received an Argus As 17A in-line engine with 185 hp and was ready to fly in the spring of 1936. The accidental first flight took place in May 1936. During taxi tests at the Gotha works airfield, the prototype suddenly took off with GWF chief pilot Hugo Harmens at the controls. When he tried to land the plane, the top-heavy machine overturned at the end of the runway. This was a preview of the poor flight characteristics of the barely controllable machine. Repaired and improved in detail, the aircraft took off for its first flight attempts in September with Harmens at the controls. Harmens found that the aircraft was very sluggish and difficult to fly, especially in curves, and tended to spin very easily. The Go 147 flight behaviour was particularly tricky during the approach. The prototype had a tendency to tip forward and thereby go into a dive. The knowledge gained from about 15 test flights was to flow into the construction of an aerodynamically refined second prototype, the Go 147 V2, with a more powerful 240-hp Argus As 10C. It was also intended to build a rotating defence stand on the rear seat. However, that did not happen. Due to the poor flight characteristics, the RLM stopped the test programme and with it, the Go 147 V2, which was under construction. As foreseen by Dr Kupper himself, the technical effort required to bring the flight characteristics of the tailless aircraft close to those of conventional aircraft was simply too high. At the same time as the Go 147 in Darmstadt-Griesheim was developed, the German Research Institute for Gliding had developed an aircraft very similar to the Go 147 in terms of its basic design, the DFS 193. This aircraft was designed by Alexander Lippisch, who is considered to be the pioneer of the tailless aircraft. Of the DFS 193, however, only a mock-up was finished. It was built by Siebel in Halle. Lippisch's best-known and series-built design was the world's first rocket aircraft, the Me 163, built by Messerschmitt in 1941. August Kupper did not live to see it. He died in an accident on 12 June 1937 in the crash of a tailless glider he had designed.

Hugo Harmens

Hugo Harmens was born in Duisburg in 1910. At the age of 18, as a mechanical engineering apprentice in Düsseldorf, he took part in the construction of a glider for the Young Pilot's group at the Düsseldorf vocational school. The first gliding flights were a key experience for Harmens, and the beginning of his flying career. He was also lucky enough to be in the right place at the right time. During a jovial round of beer at the flyers' table of the Düsseldorf Aero Club, he was selected—for

The Go 147 tailless test aircraft had unpredictable flight characteristics and was difficult to fly. (*DEHLA*)

Gotha Go 147 V1 D-IQVI before a test flight. (*DEHLA*)

whatever reason—for a free powered flight training; a training that the penniless student could have never afforded.

In 1934, Harmens became an auxiliary flight instructor at the German Aviation School (DVS) in Gotha. On 13 October 1934, he witnessed how Walter Fremd, who had switched from DVS as a works pilot to GWF, was killed in a daring flight manoeuvre that also killed a passenger. Harmens was then recruited as replacement pilot. After he was able to prove his flying skills in a spectacular demonstration flight in front of the assembled top management of the GWF, he was immediately hired as chief pilot and flight operations manager on 1 January 1935. As test pilot, Harmens carried out all of the maiden flights of the GWF in-house designs created during this time and was responsible for the setup of new aircraft. In addition, he was the company's flying poster child when it presented itself at various trade fairs or flight competitions. After the war, Harmens initially stayed in Gotha. In 1953, he was supposed to participate in the rebuilding of the GDR aviation industry in Dresden but he decided to move to the west and via Berlin he went to Düsseldorf in West Germany. Hugo Harmens never piloted an aircraft again and died in 2000.

Hugo Harmens was chief pilot and flight operations manager at GWF from 1935 to 1945. (*DEHLA*)

Gotha Go 149—Training Aircraft

The Gotha Go 149, designed by Albert Kalkert, was a single-engined training aircraft used to train fighter pilots. The RLM technical office commissioned two units in 1936. The aircraft was designed as a single-seat cabin with retractable landing gear in composite construction and a fuselage built of light alloy covered with sheet alloy. The closed cockpit had a door that could be folded up. The single-spar wings were made of wood. On the braced horizontal stabiliser, there was a rudder covered with fabric. The landing gear was pulled inwards into the wings. The Go 149 was powered by an Argus As 10C. The aircraft was intended for the beginners' training of future fighter pilots. The Go 149 V1 with the registration D-EGWF flew for the first time with chief pilot Hugo Harmens at the controls in September 1936, the second prototype with the registration D-EJFR followed two months later. However, there were no further orders from the RLM. At the Frankfurt air race in August 1938, the head of the RLM's technical office, Ernst Udet, tested the Go 149. Udet forgot to retract the landing gear and then complained about the machine's poor flight characteristics. Such are the memories of Hugo Harmens. Whether this incident played a role in the cancellation by the RLM remains speculation. GWF proposed to the ministry an armed version of the aircraft designed with a more powerful engine but there was no interest from Berlin in the Go 149 L project of a light attack and fighter aircraft—a so-called home guard. Go 149 V1 D-EGWF crash-landed at the NSFK air race in Frankfurt-am-Main in August 1939. GWF bought the crashed aircraft with serial number 885 from the RLM on 1 November 1940 at a scrap value of 100 Reichsmarks and had it scrapped—except for the engine—at its own expense.[17]

Single-seat training aircraft Gotha Go 149 V2 D-EJFR. Only two experimental versions were built. (*DEHLA*)

Ernst Udet, head of the RLM's technical office with GWF chief designer Albert Kalkert and Dr Fritz Platz, head of flight testing as they explain the Gotha Go 149. (*DEHLA*)

Ernst Udet rolls to the start with the Go 149 V1 D-EGWF. (*DEHLA*)

Gotha Go 150—The 'People's Plane'

The Gotha Go 150 was built in 1937 for the *Nationalsozialistisches Fliegerkorps* (National Socialist Flight Corps—NSFK), which had announced the need for a light powered aircraft for the retraining of glider pilots into powered flight pilots. In the two-seater aircraft with dual controls, the flight instructor and student needed to be able to sit next to each other. Albert Kalkert designed a cantilevered low-wing aircraft in constructed in wood with a three-part, single-spar wooden wing and a load-bearing plywood skin. Contrary to the single-engined design, which was customary at the time, the aircraft received two engines to increase operational safety. The fuel consumption needed to be no higher than that of a single-engined machine. The Go 150 needed to be able to continue flying in the event of an engine failure. Kalkert did without a retractable landing gear and instead chose a maintenance-friendly, rigid, one-legged landing gear. Flight instructors and students sat next to each other in a spacious, fully covered cabin with dual controls. Behind the seats was a small trunk for luggage. The aircraft was powered by two air-cooled four-cylinder in-line engines of the type Zündapp Z 9-092, each with 50-hp take-off power. The Zündapp company, known primarily for its motorcycles, had started to developed the engine in 1936 on behalf of the RLM, specifically for the needs of NSFK. The consumption was only about 12 litres of aviation fuel per 100 km. This enabled a maximum range of 800 km, which could be increased further with an additional tank in the trunk. The GWF praised the Go 150 as a 'people's aeroplane' and 'cheaper than a powerful touring car'. *Volksflugzeug*—that sounds like a cheap aeroplane for everyone; however, a fully equipped Go 150 cost between 13,000 and 14,000 Reichsmarks at the time. Influential private individuals such as the well-known German actor Heinz Rühmann actually tried, but was ultimately unsuccessful, to buy a Go 150, as these had all become state property. No new aircraft had been sold to private individuals in Germany since the spring of 1934. The state was the only customer and client for the German aviation industry. Only the *Luftwaffe*, which was still concealed at the time, *Deutsche Lufthansa*, and the air sports organisations DLV and NSFK, which were subordinate to the RLM, received new aircraft. The NSFK, founded in 1937, was the successor to the German Air Sports Association (*Deutscher Luftsportverband*—DLV), in which from 1933 all civil air sports organisations and their aircraft had been combined. With the Gotha Go 150, GWF was hoping to start building sports and touring aircraft on a large scale and to bring about a positive image change of the reputation that was badly battered in the First World War. At this time, GWF referred to their aircraft as 'The Gothas'. It was a well-known name, which, however, aroused bad memories of the infamous bomber planes of the First World War in the French and British. Now civil 'Gothas' were supposed to make positive headlines—and they did. The two prototypes of the Go 150 participated very successfully in various flying competitions and were shown at various trade fairs. On 9 July 1939, a single-seat, specially modified Go 150S set a world altitude record of 8,048 metres recognised by the international air sports association FAI. The pilot was Dr Fritz Platz, head of the Flight Testing Department at GWF. It is the only world record that an aircraft from Gotha has ever set—and it still stands today. Because the FAI changed the classification of aircraft classes after the war, the altitude record of the Go 150S is officially a historical record that can no longer be surpassed. GWF received the official confirmation of the record by the FAI in Paris on 6 December 1939.[18] By then the war in Europe had broken out and there was no longer any need for a possible mass production. Fighter aircraft, such as the licence production of the Messerschmitt Bf 110 or the construction of gliders, now had priority in production. Nevertheless, when all was said and done, in addition to the two prototypes, Gotha also delivered a small production series of ten Go 150s to the NSFK by mid-1940. One example remained in GWF's inventory and was taken over as a company aircraft in 1941. In September 1944, the RLM still had ten Go 150s in its aircraft inventory. However, they were rarely used. That month, these aircraft completed 15 flights with a total of only one hour of flight time. From May 1944, the University of Jena used a machine as a test aircraft for a secret research project. Several Go 150 fell into the hands of the Allies at the end of the war and it is said that some of them were even flown afterwards. Not a single one of these aircraft survived.

Press photo of the Gotha Go 150: The sport and touring aircraft was developed for the National Socialist Air Corps (NSFK) starting in 1937. (*Author's collection*)

Oskar Ursinus had Albert Kalkert explain the Go 150 to him at the NSFK air race in August 1938 in Frankfurt-am-Main. Kalkert and Ursinus knew each other from gliding at the Wasserkuppe. (*DEHLA*)

Gotha, 5 July 1939, 7:35 a.m.: The Go 150S, specially modified for the world record flight, rolls to take off. (*Adelheid Krajewski-Platz*)

'Fought for every metre': Dr Fritz Platz, head of the Flight Testing Department, carried out the world record flight of the Go 150. His wife, Angela Platz, on the right with a bouquet of flowers. (*Adelheid Krajewski-Platz*)

Gotha Go 241—Touring Plane

Believing that the war that broke out in September 1939 would only last for a short time, the GWF management hoped for a rapid increase in demand for civilian aircraft after the war ended quickly. That is the reason why Albert Kalkert designed a modern and much more comfortable successor to the Go 150—the Gotha Go 241—in 1940, presumably without an official order from the technical office. The four-seater aircraft constructed from wood had a retractable landing gear and was equipped with two Hirth HM 506 A in-line engines with 160 hp each. This enabled the aircraft to reach a top speed of 275 kph, and the range was 800 km. Since the war continued unabated, and the aircraft had not been officially requested, all hopes for a series production of the Go 241 were dashed. GWF probably used the prototype with the identification D-IRMM itself and used it for courier services. In 1944, the aircraft was destroyed in an American air raid on the GWF factory premises.

Unique piece: The four-seater Gotha Go 241 touring aircraft was designed by Albert Kalkert in 1940 as the successor to the Go 150. (*Author's collection*)

Gotha Go 242—Cargo Glider

The Gotha Go 242 was developed as an enlarged addition to the DFS 230 cargo glider and was not only suitable for transporting troops, but also for supplies. In mid-1940, the RLM commissioned GWF to build two prototypes. At the same time as the GWF, the *Deutsche Forschungsanstalt für Segelflug* (German Research Institute for Glider Flight—DFS) was also commissioned to develop a prototype. Since the DFS did not have its own production capability, the prototype of the DFS 331 was also to be built at GWF. This created the curious situation that two competing models were developed and built in parallel in Gotha. The designers at GWF under Albert Kalkert designed a high-wing aircraft with a covered tubular steel fuselage, wooden wings and a twin vertical tail stabiliser assembly with an intermediate loading ramp that opened upwards. On 9 November 1941, Hugo Harmens carried out the maiden Go 242 V1 flight. It took place just under a month after the competitor model DFS 331. In January, the prototype was transferred to the E-Stelle (test centre) in Rechlin and tested. After the successful testing, the RLM decided to start series production for more than the initially confirmed 20-machine series. The second prototype, Go 242 V2, was completed in February 1942 and transferred to Rechlin. During high-speed testing, the weakly constructed tail assembly broke. The pilot, Hugo Harmens, was able to parachute himself with great difficulty from the crashing plane. His technician, however, was killed in the accident. The first production model after the initial production series of 20 Go 242 A-0s was the Go 242 A-1 version with landing skids and a removable landing gear. The Go 242 A-2 had an additional coupling under the loading ramp. This enabled either a braking parachute to be installed or two of the cargo gliders to be pulled by a tow plane. The Go 242 B-1 had a fixed, brake-able three-wheel chassis with a nose wheel. There was also a motorised variant of the glider, the Gotha Go 244 B-1. Since the model did not catch on, GWF upgraded many of these transporters back to the Go 242 B-1. The successor model, the Go 242 B-2, had a cantilevered undercarriage with lateral supports on the fuselage. 256 units left the factory. The following version, Go 242 B-3, had side doors. The projected variations, B-4 and B-5, were most likely never completed. The Go 242 C-1, which had a buoyant fuselage, was designed for special missions. The main producer of the Go 242 was the Hartwig company in Sonneberg. In Gotha, only the 20 units of the initial production series were made. The last Go 242 were delivered in March 1943. Mainly, the air force used the glider for supply flights, although it was occasionally used for paratrooper missions. The plan was for the grounded Go 242s to be dismantled and then brought back to safety for renewed use. As it happened, many ended up as one-way transports to supply trapped troops on the Eastern Front. The crews then had to fight their way back to their own lines alongside the Wehrmacht. By 1944, around 1,500 Go 242s had left the production facilities in Sonneberg and Gotha.

The significantly larger Go 242 was intended to complement the DFS 230 cargo glider. In the picture is a pre-production model Go 242 A-0. (*Dlugosch collection*)

Two Gotha Go 242s in flight. (*DEHLA*)

Lattice fuselage of a Go 242 C in the German Museum of Technology in Berlin. Many Go 242s ended up as one-way transporters on the Eastern Front. (*Author's collection*)

Gotha Go 244—Transport Aircraft

Starting in 1941, GWF developed the Go 244, a motorised version of the Go 242 cargo glider. With this construction, a final, independent design could be produced in series. The construction of the Go 242 was designed from the outset so that it could be motorised without any problems. Even in the construction phase consideration was given to the idea of installing an Argus As 10 engine in the bow of the fuselage in order to enable the cargo glider to return on its own power. However, calculations showed that the engine would have been too weak for that purpose. Therefore, two Gnome-Rhône 14M radial engines from French stocks, each with 740 hp, were installed in front of the two tail girders. In the summer of 1941, the first two prototypes of the motorised Go 242 were under construction. To better distinguish it from the non-motorised version, it was given the designation Go 244. Starting on 10 January 1942, the second prototype, the Go 244 V2, was transferred to the testing site in Rechlin. However, the two Gnome-Rhône radial engines also turned out to be too weak. After a test shutdown of a motor, the machine could not stay in the air. Other than that, the E-Stelle did not find any serious deficiencies. This was a fatal misjudgement that appeared in later use. Series production of the transporter started in Gotha. The first machines delivered to the troops were designated Go 244 B-1, as they had taken over the axle chassis of the Go 242 B-1. The Gotha Go 244 A-1 was apparently not produced. Neither was the Go 244 A-2, which was projected to use two Russian Shvetsov M-25 engines.

Gotha Go 244: The motorised version of the cargo glider Go 242 did not prove itself, many Go 244 were upgraded to cargo gliders. (*Dlugosch collection*)

The army made modifications to the machine to improve the launch characteristics but that did not help much either. The defects of the Go 244 transporter were already evident after the first few missions. The aircraft were used with Luftflotte 4 in the southern section of the Eastern Front. Here a complete transport unit was equipped with the Go 244. Within three weeks, between 21 June and 10 July 1942, the unit recorded 75 emergency landings and several serious accidents due to overloading and incorrect loading. Luftflotte 4 then imposed an immediate take-off ban. Field Marshal Erhard Milch, general aircraft supervisor and head of the technical office at the RLM, considered the Go 244 'a faulty design due to its short range and limited possibilities for use'. He made serious accusations towards the people responsible for rating the aircraft positively and those who did not recognise the aircraft's weaknesses.[19] The RLM then stopped the further construction of the Go 244. The construction of the further developed versions Go 244 B-3 and B-5 were also stopped. A number of Go 244s equipped back into the Go 242 glider.

9

Aircraft Produced Under Licence

Heinkel He 45 and He 46—Reconnaissance Aircraft

On 1 January 1934, GWF received an order from the RLM to manufacture 48 Heinkel He 45s and 50 He 46s under licence. The production of these aircraft in Gotha got off to a very slow start because the organisational and technical requirements for aircraft construction in Gotha first had to be created. This is probably why the repair of these two aircraft was started before the actual production commenced.

The He 45c—the name of the Gotha construction licence for the He 45b with the BMW VI—12-cylinder in-line engine with 600 hp, was an armed two-seater biplane with composite construction that was used by the *Luftwaffe* as a reconnaissance aircraft and light bomber.

A total of 87 Heinkel He 45c are said to have been built in Gotha, 40 of which were given to the Franco's air force in Spain. On 11 December 1936, GWF signed a licence agreement with Ernst Heinkel Flugzeugwerke AG for the construction of the Heinkel He 45 and He 46, presumably a supplement to the aircraft delivered from 1934 onwards.[20]

According to the delivery statistics of GWF from 5 May 1938, the last He 45c was delivered in June 1937 and production was switched to the He 46.[21] The two-seater close-range reconnaissance aircraft was a composite construction. It was a high-wing aircraft, braced with struts, and had an air-cooled nine-cylinder radial engine SAM 22B with 600 hp. A total of around 36 machines of this type are said to have been built in Gotha by 1938. Among them were at least four, probably even six, of the unarmed version He 46 D with SAM 22B engines, which were intended for the *Luftwaffe*. All other machines were exported to Hungary. The machine designated as He 46 E received the Hungarian licence version of the French radial engine Gnome-Rhône 14K with an output of 1,020 hp. During the transfer of an He 46 to Hungary, the head of GWF flight control Richard Schade and a technician had a fatal accident near Hof, in Bavaria.

Heinkel He 45c at the GWF works airfield. The aircraft was built in Gotha until June 1937. (*DEHLA*)

GWF licence construction: Close-range reconnaissance aircraft Heinkel He 46 D before delivery to the air force. (*DEHLA*)

German Research Institute for Gliding DFS 230—Cargo Glider

The cargo glider DFS 230 was developed in 1936 by Hans Jacobs from the German Research Institute for Gliding in Darmstadt. The maiden flight took place in 1937. In November 1938, the RLM entrusted GWF with 'the production-ready redesign' of the glider. The prototype DFS 230 V5, which was simplified for mass production in Gotha, was completed in March 1939. The aircraft was a braced high-wing aircraft in composite construction, with a covered tubular steel fuselage and wooden wings. In addition to the pilot, there was room for nine paratroopers in the glider. A total 72 DFS 230 aircraft, versions A-2, A-3, and B-2, were built in Gotha. Most of the 1600 to 1942 DFS 230s were produced in the Robert Hartwig wood and toy factory in Sonneberg, in southern Thuringia. The DFS 230s were used for the first time on a grand scale in 1940 when the Belgian fort Eben-Emael was conquered and in 1941 when Crete was invaded. After that, they were mostly used as one-way transporters in North Africa and on the Eastern Front. Starting in January 1944, production of the DFS 230 was to be resumed. An improved version with a wider fuselage and a fixed take-off and landing gear in place of the skids was provided for this version. The prototype of this version, known as the DFS 230 C-1, was built and tested by GWF as the DFS 230 V6, in December 1943. However, a total of only 12 DFS 230 C-1s left the 'Mraz' factory in occupied Czechoslovakia. In 1944, an improved version of the cargo glider, customised for the Junkers Ju 388 tow plane, was built in Gotha. The DFS 230 V7 was to serve as a design model for the DFS 230 E version. However, in comparison to the cargo glider Kalkert Ka 430, designed by the former GWF chief designer Albert Kalkert who was at the *Mitteldeutsche Metallwerke* in Erfurt, the DFS 230 V7, with its side doors and overhead loading hatch, which was a nuisance to load, had no chance. The prototype was then used by GWF to test a new tow variant, the lift tow.

DFS 230 V5: This simplified prototype, built in Gotha in March 1939, was the design model for the mass-produced DFS 230 A-1. (*DEHLA*)

In 1944, GWF further developed the DFS 230 cargo glider. However, the cargo glider DFS 230 V7 could not prevail against the competing Ka 430 of the former Gotha chief designer Albert Kalkert. In any case, there was no longer any need for gliders. (*Dlugosch collection*)

The prototype of the DFS 230 V7 was the design model for the DFS 230 E. (*Dlugosch collection*)

German Research Institute for Glider Flight DFS 331—Cargo Glider

After the successful use of the DFS 230 against Belgium in the summer of 1940, the General Staff demanded a larger successor to the glider. As with the DFS 230, Hans Jacobs was commissioned with the design. Curiously, the three prototypes designated as DFS 331 were built at GWF, which, at the same time developed its own competing cargo glider, the Gotha Go 242. The DFS 331 was a high-wing aircraft in composite construction with a double vertical stabiliser, which, in addition to the pilot, could accommodate 18 paratroopers who could get out through the side doors. The maiden flight of the first prototype, the DFS 331 V1, was carried out by the well-known German record pilot Hanna Reitsch while being towed by a Ju 52 on 30 September 1940 from the airfield of the Gotha Air Base. Over 100 successful tow flights are said to have been carried out by January 1941. The DFS 331 V1 showed good flight characteristics, so the RLM ordered an initial production series of 20 machines, which were then to be manufactured in the *Reparaturwerk Erfurt* (REWE—later called the *Mitteldeutsche Metallwerke*). The designer of the Go 242, Albert Kalkert, who had left GWF on 1 October 1940, had, in the meantime started working at REWE. The construction of the DFS 331 V2 and then the V3 were also supposed to take place here. However, the completion of the prototypes and the production of the initial production series machines were so delayed that the RLM ultimately decided on the GWF model. In that time, the Go 242 V1 had been successfully tested at the E-Stelle in Rechlin. The RLM then decided to start series production of the Go 242 and on 24 March 1941, ordered the suspension of all work on the DFS cargo glider.

The cargo glider DFS 331 was created as an enlarged addition to the DFS 230. Three prototypes were built at GWF. (*Krieg collection*)

Focke-Wulf Fw 58 'Weihe'—Training and Liaison Aircraft

The twin-engined low-wing aircraft, covered with fabric and metal and equipped with a retractable landing gear, was developed in 1934 by Focke-Wulf in Bremen. It was produced for the training of pilots, bomb aimers, and radio operators in the *Luftwaffe*. In addition to training, the versatile and robust aircraft was also used as a light transport, liaison, and as an ambulance aircraft. The maiden flight of the Fw 58 V1 with the registration D-ABEM took place on 18 January 1935. The RLM commissioned GWF to take over the licensed production of the aircraft. The contract with Focke-Wulf is dated 30 June 1936.[22] Starting in 1937, up to 158 training aircraft of the type Fw 58 C-2 with a covered nose and equipped with two As 10C engines were built in Gotha and handed over to the air force.

In 1942, another small production series of twelve Fw 58 G-1 ambulance aircraft with two stretchers followed.

Starting in 1937, 158 Focke-Wulf Fw 58 C-2 training aircraft were built under licence in Gotha. (*DEHLA*)

This Fw 58 C-2, which was probably also built in Gotha, was photographed at a flight day in Gotha. (*Dlugosch collection*)

Messerschmitt Bf 110 B, C, F, G—Heavy Fighter and Night Fighter

In 1934, the RLM commissioned several aircraft companies to develop a heavy fighter, a destroyer. The companies Bayerische Flugzeugwerke (BFW), Focke-Wulf, and Henschel were involved. The BFW (renamed Messerschmitt AG starting in 1938) prevailed in the competition with their design, the two-seat all-metal low-wing Bf 110. The maiden flight of the prototype took place on 12 May 1936 in Augsburg. As early as the end of 1936, the RLM commissioned GWF as a licensee for this model. The licence agreement for the Messerschmitt Bf 110 B-1, the first production model with a Jumo 210 in-line engine, is dated 4 July 1938.[23] Large-scale production began in Gotha at the end of 1938 and a total of 62 Messerschmitt Bf 110 B-1s were built by October 1939. One month later, the further developed Bf 110 C-1 with more powerful Daimler Benz DB 601 engines replaced the Bf 110 B-1 in production. With the exception of the Bf 110 D, all further developments of the twin-engined fighter aircraft were built in Gotha. Starting in June 1941, Messerschmitt withdrew from production of the Bf 110 entirely, and all aircraft of this type produced from this point on were made exclusively in Gotha and at the Luther works in Braunschweig. GWF thus became the main producer and was also responsible for their further development. Production of the Bf 110 was shut down in 1942 in favour of the successor model, the Messerschmitt Me 210, but when the Me 210 flopped, the GWF had to restart production of the predecessor model. After the end of the series Bf 110 E and F, the Bf 110 G entered series production at the end of 1942. The prototype of the G variant was completed in Gotha in June 1942. GWF delivered almost 1,500 units of the night fighter variant Bf 110 G-4 alone by 1945, more than any other version of this aircraft. From mid-1944, GWF was actually planning to produce the single-engined Focke-Wulf Fw 190 and the successor model Ta 152, but the Bf 110 was still manufactured until the end of the war. A total of 2,744 Bf 110s, of all the versions built there, left the Gotha factory halls, which was almost half of all machines of this type ever produced. By the end of 1944, GWF was to have completed two Bf 110 model aircraft for the planned H series with two DB 603 E engines.[24] It was never determined if the two aircraft were actually being built, as the further development of the Bf 110 was halted in November 1944 when the RLM launched the *Jägernotprogramm* (fighter emergency programme).

Wing construction and fuselage completion of the Messerschmitt Bf 110 in Hall 101 of GWF. (*Dlugosch collection*)

Aircraft Produced Under Licence

Final assembly in Hall 100. Almost half of all Bf 110s were built here. (*Dlugosch collection*)

The Messerschmitt Bf 110 in various versions was built in Gotha from 1938 to 1945. (*DEHLA*)

Messerschmitt Me 210—Heavy Fighter and Fighter Bomber

The Messerschmitt Me 210 was the successor to the Bf 110, a twin-engined, two-seater multi-purpose fighter aircraft. Starting in 1942, series production was to start in Gotha and replace the Bf 110. The production facilities in Gotha were converted to the new model, the material was cut and GWF employees at Messerschmitt were retrained to produce the new model. Then, surprisingly, the RLM announced the end of the Me 210 on 9 March 1942. Due to design defects, the model had proven to be a complete failure during testing and in use, so much so that the RLM was forced to pull the emergency brake. Nevertheless, at least one, probably even two Me 210 A-1s were assembled in Gotha from the delivered components from Messerschmitt. The use of a Me 210 built in Gotha with *Kampfgeschwader 6* (KG 6—Fighter Squadron 6), which was stationed on the French Channel coast, was confirmed. On 6 September 1942, during a mission over southern England, the serial number 3257, along with another Me 210, was shot down by two British Hawker Typhoons.[24] In Gotha, production of the predecessor Bf 110 had long since started again. Apart from the loss of time during which production was idle, the production changeover resulted in costs of 7.1 million Reichsmarks, for which GWF invoiced the RLM. For comparison: a delivered Bf 110 C, depending on the equipment, cost around 158,000 Reichsmarks.[14]

Only one or two machines of the heavy fighter Messerschmitt Me 210 were built in Gotha from the delivered components in 1942. (*DEHLA*)

Messerschmitt Me 328—Flying Bomb

In June 1944, the RLM decided to transfer the production of the single-seat Messerschmitt Me 328 fighter to GWF. Starting in 1941, the aircraft had been developed as a non-powered glider by Messerschmitt AG and the German Research Institute for Gliding (DFS). The maiden flight took place on 3 August 1942 in Ainring by the test pilot Hanna Reitsch. In addition to the non-powered variant, which was designated as Me 328 A, there was also the Me 328 B variant, which was driven by two Argus As 014 pulse jet engine. However, the two pulse jet engines caused strong vibrations, which led to damage to the structure of the aircraft. The test programme was significantly delayed and there were only a few test flights. At the beginning of 1944, the idea came up to use aircraft equipped with a bombload in 'full deployment'—that is, as a loss device against the expected invasion fleet of the Allies. The Me 328, which was relatively cheap to produce, also came into focus again. The plan was to bring an explosive-filled and manned Me 328 A pulled by a tow plane—presumably in the lift tow researched in Gotha—to the invasion fleet. Shortly before the target area, the pilot of the Me 328 was supposed to detach himself from the tow plane, glide towards the target and try to jump out of the machine at the last moment before the explosive charge detonated. Ultimately, the RLM then decided to man the Fieseler Fi 103 (V1) flying bomb for this purpose and to convert it for self-sacrifice operations. Therefore, the Me 328 was not built under licence in Gotha.

The Me 328 B, equipped with two Argus As 014 pulse jet engines, was to be used as a flying bomb against the Allied invasion fleet. (*Dr Koos collection*)

Focke-Wulf Ta 152 H-1—High-Altitude Fighter Aircraft

The single-seat Focke-Wulf Ta 152 fighter aircraft was a further development of the Focke-Wulf Fw 190 D. The maiden flight of the prototype Fw 190 V33/U1 took place on 13 July 1944. Powered by a liquid-cooled V-12 in-line Jumo 213 E-1 engine with 1,750 take-off horsepower, the Ta 152 reached a top speed of almost 760 kph at an altitude of 12,500 metres. This made the Ta 152 at least as good as, if not superior, to the Allied opponents in terms of performance. Starting in December 1944, GWF was to switch production to the new model and in March 1945 to deliver the first two copies of the Ta 152 H-1/R11. The Ta 152 H-1/R11 version was specially developed for high-altitude hunting and, in addition to a pressurised cabin and extended wings, also had two additional injection systems with which the engine's output could briefly be increased. Setbacks in the testing of the prototypes and the catastrophic war situation led to the delayed start of series production. In addition to GWF, other German aircraft plants, including the Mitteldeutsche Metallwerke in neighbouring Erfurt, were also involved. GWF was to finish assembling the first two Ta 152s in March 1945, and by September 1945 production was then to be gradually increased to up to 70 machines per month. According to the industrial delivery plan of 25 February 1945, a total of 600 Ta 152s were to be delivered by 1946. GWF was supposed to manufacture the wings itself and also to supply them to another licensee such as Erla Maschinenwerke GmbH in Leipzig. The Hartwig company in Sonneberg was also to be involved in

This captured Ta 152 H-0 was shipped to the USA in 1945 and is the only surviving example in the world. (*USAF*)

production. The wooden tail assemblies of the Ta 152 were to be built there. When the US troops occupied Gotha on 4 April 1945, they found components for five Ta 152s that had not yet been assembled. A few machines of the pre-production version Focke-Wulf Ta 152 H-0, which were not yet equipped with the two injection systems, were given to Jagdgeschwader 301 (Fighter Squadron 301) and also scored a few kills with this high-performance fighter in the final phase of the war.

Horten Ho 229—Flying Wing Jet Fighter

The Horten H IX, later referred to as the Ho 229, was the design of a single-seater flying wing fighter with jet propulsion that the brothers Reimar and Walter Horten presented to the RLM. The Horten brothers from Bonn made a name for themselves in the 1930s with the construction of tailless gliders. Reichsmarschall Hermann Göring is said to have been enthusiastic about the design, but required a range of 1,000 km, a bombload of 1,000 kg, and a top speed of 1,000 kph. The first prototype, the H IX V1, which was still built as a glider and which flew for the first time on 1 March 1944, was created in the Luftwaffe Command IX in Göttingen, which was founded specifically for this purpose. Since the Hortens did not have their own production capacities, the RLM transferred the series production of around 100 copies of the flying wing, which was then equipped with two jet engines to GWF. The aircraft was constructed as a composite construction, consisting of a steel pipe fuselage covered with wood and wooden wings. All cargo gliders designed and built in Gotha up to 1944 were created using this construction method. After the end of the glider production, GWF's experience with composite constructions was probably the reason why the factory in Gotha was commissioned for the Horton project. Starting at the end of June 1944, in order to transfer the technology, and to get an overview of the construction, several of the engineers in Gotha were sent to Göttingen. On 10 September 1944, GWF received the order from the newly created *Amt der technischen Luftrüstung* (TLR—Technical Air Armament Office) to prepare the series production of the aircraft now known as the Ho 229 and to create a dummy model. This model was the preliminary stage for the first prototype that was close to being ready for series production, the Ho 229 V6, and was constantly modified. Project management in Gotha was taken over by GWF's chief designer, Albert Hünerjäger, and his deputy Walter Wundes.

Just one month later, on 13 October 1944, a first working meeting took place on the 'largely completed' dummy model with Lieutenant Brüning, the man in charge of overseeing the model for the *E-Stelle* Rechlin (Rechlin test centre). After that, the Gotha designers had to work through a long list of defects. On 25 October 1944, the issue of the installation of the engines was the subject of another meeting with engineers from the Rechlin electrical engineering department. After inspecting a dummy engine of the Jumo 004, the engineers found that the installation of this engine in the Ho 229 was not 'considered possible'. The main reason was that the engines were not sealed off from the airframe, which would have been necessary for fire protection reasons. To change the jet engines, which were still very prone to failure at the time, and had a short life expectancy, the entire middle section of the aircraft would have to be dismantled. After the viewing appointment, it was decided to build the significantly narrower and more compact BMW 003 engines into the dummy model. BMW was to provide GWF with a dummy engine for this. After another meeting between the E-Stelle Rechlin, Horten and GWF on 23 November 1944, it was 'conclusively decided' that Gotha should also take over the prototype construction of the Ho 229 V3, V4, and V5, in accordance to the 'Göttingen version'. These three prototypes were planned as pure flight test vehicles without armament. In contrast to the second prototype, Ho 229 V2, which was currently under construction in Göttingen, they were to receive a modified landing gear, an ejection seat and static reinforcements in the mid-section, in the wing and in the rudders. The Jumo engine, which was to be installed in a relocated arrangement, could still be used as the power plant. It is not known why the V3 to V5 were not structurally adapted to the development status of the V6 in the Gotha version. It was odd, because parallel to this, the construction work on the V6 was also to be carried out 'as quickly as possible', so that 'the V6 can be manufactured after the V5 without any pause in between'.[25] For the V6 and the following test aircraft, the middle section, in which the cockpit and the engines were located, was to be completely redesigned. In addition to thickening the profile by 17.5 per cent, a pressurised cabin was to be included. The Jumo 004 was still an option, but the two engines were to be moved 140 mm further outwards. 'According to these drafts, a dummy model with and without a pressurized cabin is to be created immediately.'[25] It is not entirely clear whether GWF then converted the existing dummy model for the V6 or built a completely new dummy model. With these changes, it would have a completely different appearance compared to the V2 and also the V3 to V5. In the meantime, in December 1944, the first jet-powered prototype, the Horten Ho 229 V2, was finished in Göttingen. On 2 February 1945, test pilot Erwin Ziller successfully took off on his maiden flight from Oranienburg near Berlin. During another test flight on 19 February, one of the two Jumo engines failed at an altitude of around 800 metres. Ziller tried in vain to get the engine going again. The flying wing flew out of control and crashed.

Ziller was fatally injured in the impact when he was thrown from the cockpit. Meanwhile, the other prototypes were being built in Friedrichroda, 15 km from Gotha. GWF had relocated prototype construction there, to the Ortlepp Furniture Joinery, after the devastating US air raids on the Gotha factory premises in February and July 1944. On 6 February 1945, US bombers also attacked Friedrichroda. The joinery and prototype construction just barely escaped destruction. A bomb hit the Ortlepp family's house right next to the production hall, wiping out a five-person refugee family from Wuppertal who had found refuge there. On 22 February 1945, a new viewing of the V6 dummy was set, for which Lieutenant Brüning travelled once more to Friedrichroda. This time, too, Brüning found serious defects that still had to be remedied. The pilot bumped his head against the pilot's cowl when his seat parachute was attached. In addition, the ejection seat could be deployed without the canopy having to be thrown off beforehand. The date for the elimination of these and other defects was the next meeting on 5 March 1945.[26] There was no longer any talk of building series aircraft. Instead, GWF received the order to build, 'in addition to the 3 V models V3 to V5 in the V2 version (Göttingen version), 10 further (experimental) aircraft V6 to V15' (in the Gotha version). In the meantime, GWF had also submitted its own design for a flying wing jet fighter to the RLM with the Gotha P-60 project. There was not much time left to implement these projects. On 4 April 1945, US troops reached Gotha and occupied the largely destroyed wagon factory. Four days later they also entered Friedrichroda. In the Ortlepp Joinery, they captured the relatively complete middle section of the Ho 229 V3 and two fuselage frames of the Ho 229 in different stages of construction, the V4 and V5. In the GWF branch in Ilmenau, they discovered another destroyed fuselage structure of the flying wing, presumably it was the dummy of the Ho 229 V6 in the 'Gotha version'. A French slave labourer led the Americans to the buried construction documents of the GWF. These included drawings and correspondence in regards to various Ho 229 prototypes up to the V9. At the Hartwig company in Sonneberg, the Americans found an incomplete and an almost complete set of wings for the Ho 229. Together with the Ho 229 V3 in the 'Göttingen version', the wings were brought to the USA as loot and have been preserved to this day.

On 8 April 1945, US troops found several unfinished prototypes of the Horten Ho 229 at the Ortlepp joinery workshop in Friedrichroda. The picture probably shows the Ho 229 V3. (*USAF*)

Rear view of the Ho 229. GWF had relocated prototype construction to the joinery in Friedrichroda. (*USAF*)

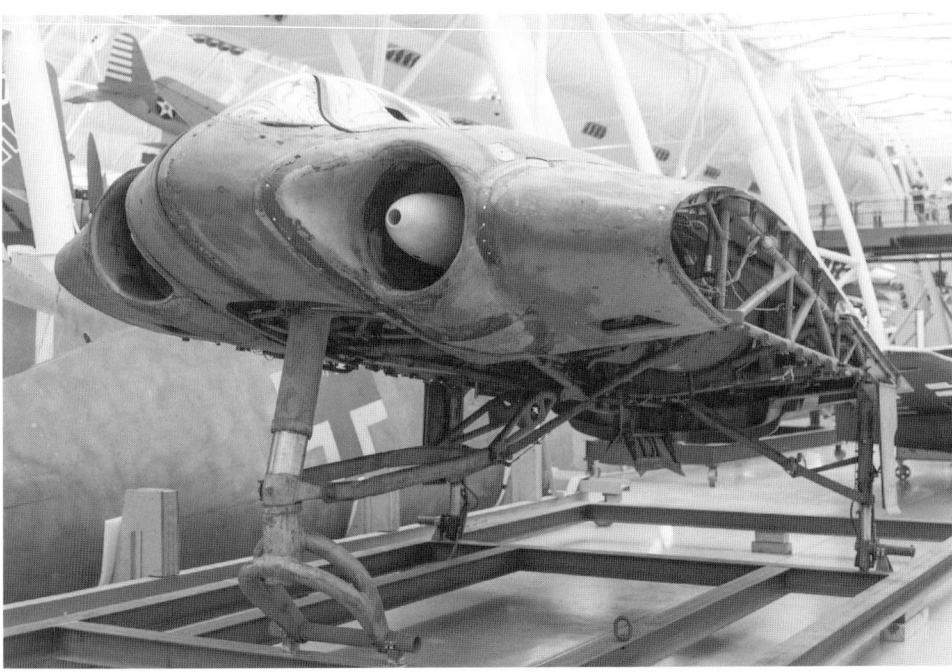

Horten Ho 229 captured in Friedrichroda, has been exhibited at the Steven F. Udvar-Hazy Center in Chantilly, Virginia, since September 2017. (*Dr Andreas Zeitler*)

10

Projects 1935–1945

In addition to the samples that were put into series production, the GWF design department worked on many other projects that mostly only existed on paper and about which relatively little is known. Since these drafts were mostly created without an official commission from the RLM, they rarely went beyond the planning status. Up until 1939, there were various designs of civil sport and touring aircraft, but also of military machines such as destroyers or light fighters. After the Go 242 production was phased out in early 1943 (the last Go 242s delivered were retrofitted Go 244s), GWF only built the Messerschmitt Bf 110 under licence. The management was interested in rebuilding a design office and bringing their in-house designs back into play. Starting in 1941–42, under the new aerodynamicist Rudolf Göthert, replacement solutions for the cargo glider Go 242 and the Go 244 transporter were developed. Starting at the end of 1944, projects for in-house designed flying wings, as an alternative to the Horten Ho 229, which was built under licence, were developed. Many documents and records that the Americans found, not only in Gotha but also at other aircraft manufacturers in April 1945, were returned to the West German Federation of the *Bundesverband der Deutschen Luft- und Raumfahrtindustrie* (BDLI— German Aerospace Industries Association) in the mid-1960s. The Gotha files, which had been inaccessible up until this point, found their worldwide distribution from there. This the reason why documents about the Gotha Wagon Factory are still scattered all over Germany today. Because of this, only a few original sources on GWF projects were available for this book. The source for most of the information was secondary literature. The Gotha P-60 and the lift tow projects, from which original documents could be evaluated, are an exception.

Cargo Glider Projects

As the successor to the cargo glider Go 242, which was still designed under the direction of Albert Kalkert, GWF presented various other solutions to the RLM. Like the Go 242, all of these projects were to be carried out in a composite construction, with a covered tubular steel fuselage and wooden wings. One of these projects was the Gotha P-47, a cargo glider with a central fuselage and loading ramp that, in contrast to the Go 242, could also be opened in flight. Since the project obviously did not convince the RLM, the GWF design engineers looked at the Go 242 again.

They tried to improve the machine by converting the glider to a central fuselage without the twin vertical stabiliser. Photographs suggest that the non-airworthy dummy model was only used for loading tests. It is not known whether the machine was further developed. Another design draft is the P-50/1, a so-called storm cargo glider in a canard construction style with a large loading ramp that could carry a weapon in addition to paratroopers. The second project under this name was the P-50/2, a high-wing aircraft with a loading ramp. Finally, the P-52 was a cargo glider amphibian that was supposed to land on the water and then head for the coast with an auxiliary engine. Lastly, the P-53 was designed; a high-wing aircraft with landing gear and nose flap, which then probably led to the development of the Go 345.

The Gotha Go 242 with a central fuselage was obviously only used for loading tests. The dummy was not airworthy. (*DEHLA*)

Gotha Go 345—Storm Cargo Glider

The most advanced cargo glider project was the Go 345. The design started at the end of 1943 under the new aerodynamicist Rudolf Göthert. The high-winged, composite construction consisted of a tubular steel fuselage covered with plywood, wooden wings, and tail assembly. Two versions were designed. The Go 345 A version was to have the Go 242's front nose that could be folded up for loading and unloading. In contrast, the Go 345 B had a long nose with a cockpit for the two-man crew. In the fuselage, there was space for a 3,200-kg payload or ten paratroopers who could get out of the Go 345 B via side doors or on the Go 345 A via a bow section that could be opened up. A motorised version with two Argus As 014 pulse jet engines under the wings was also planned. After uncoupling from the tow plane, the glider was to dive for the target. Some 600 metres above the target point, a braking parachute was supposed to slow the aircraft down. In the Go 345 B, a brake rocket was also provided in the bow section in front of the cockpit, which could be ignited shortly before the impact on the ground. The tip of the fuselage itself should then act like a kind of crumple zone and completely slow down the impact. In July 1944, wind tunnel tests were carried out on a model of the Go 345 in Braunschweig. A prototype, the Go 345 V1, and probably even a second, was under construction when the project was discontinued in the autumn of 1944. The further development of a nose first, point-landing aircraft was planned with the P-53Z project, but it too never came to fruition.

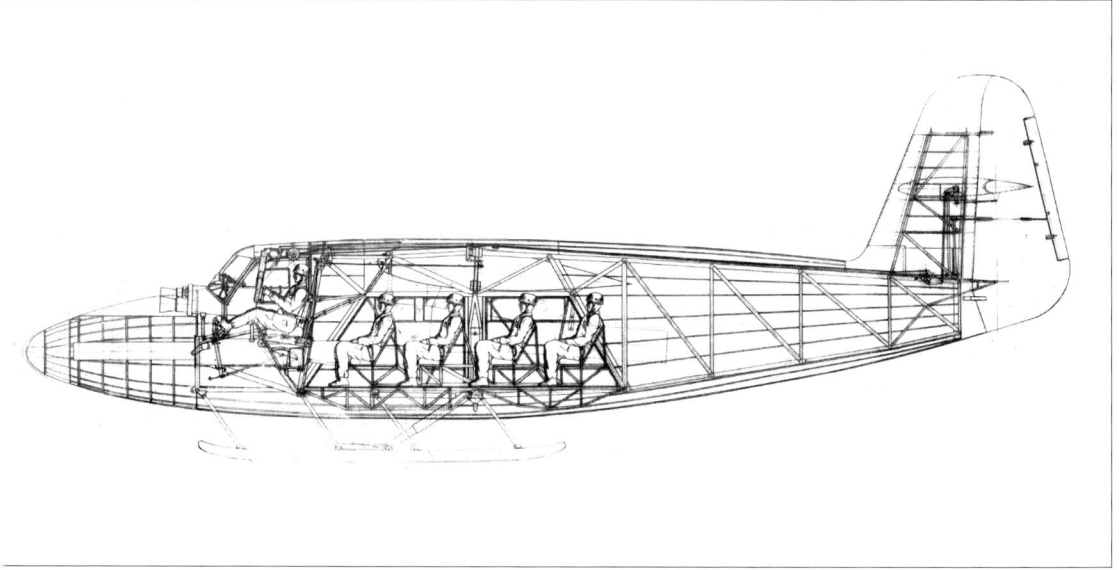

The development of the cargo glider Go 345 was halted in the autumn of 1944 after the first prototype was almost finished. (*DEHLA*)

Projects to Replace the Go 244

Even while the first Go 244 was still being delivered, the General Staff asked for a successor to the transporter. GWF proposed several drafts to the RLM, but they were all rejected. One of these projects was the P-35, a high-wing aircraft with a twin vertical tail stabiliser assembly similar to the Go 244. Two Bramo 323 radial engines were to serve as propulsion. The P-39 was even bigger; the project was to be equipped with three Bramo 323s. One motor should be attached to the fuselage, the other two in the wings. The design was considered a light transport aircraft. With the Gotha P-40B, GWF once again planned an asymmetrical aircraft with two fuselages, almost 25 years after the Gotha G VI. The crew of the high-wing aircraft sat in their own fuselage with an engine and a cantilevered, asymmetrical tail assembly. Connected via the wing, there was a removable second fuselage as a load container to the right. At the same time, the GWF designers also continued to develop the Go 244. As the P-45 and P-46, it was to be equipped with a single central fuselage engine, Jumo 211, with either a single or double tail assembly. For reasons unknown, this project was not pursued any further.

Attempts to 'Lift Tow'

Starting in March 1944, the GWF's design department tested out a new method of towing cargo gliders, the so-called lift tow. Compared to the conventional method, in which the glider was pulled by a rope attached to the tail of the powered aircraft, the designers now used two tow ropes that were connected to each other via tow couplings in the wings. As a result, the glider lifted itself over the tow plane after take-off with a rope angle of about 30 degrees. The towed aircraft was controlled via electrical wires within the tow ropes. These formed a closed circuit that could be interrupted by either of the two pilots. In this case, ignition cartridges were automatically triggered in the tow couplings, which separated the team from each other. A Junkers Ju 87 and the cargo glider DFS 210 V6 served as the experimental team.[27] The GWF engineers, headed by aerodynamicist Rudolf Göthert, found in their tests that the flight behaviour was more stable than the normal procedure. The climbing performance of the attached aircraft was also significantly better. The new method also made it possible to tow unmanned aerial vehicles, which gave the GWF designers new ideas. The towing test attempts were interrupted on 20 July 1944 by a USAAF bombing raid on GWF, in which the test combination of Ju 87 and DFS 230 V6 was destroyed.

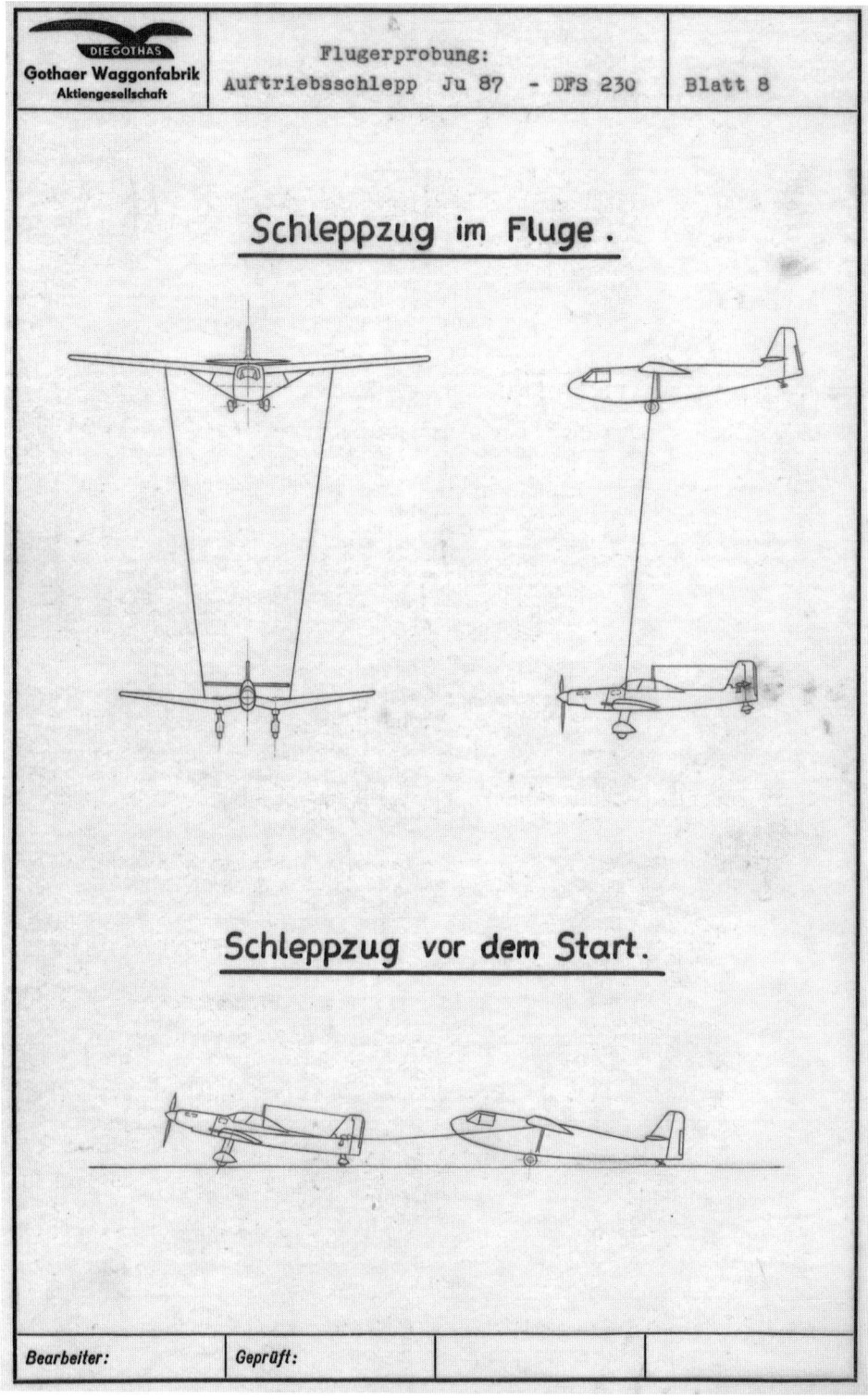

To test the lift tow, GWF used a Junkers Ju 87 as a tow plane and the cargo glider DFS 230 V6, later also the DFS 230 V7. (*DEHLA*)

P-56, P-57, P-58 Lift-Tow Projects

After the successful tests of the lift tow, GWF's design department designed several partially unmanned trailer aircraft for various uses. This included the project of a fuel carrier, which was carried out under the project name Gotha P-56. The P-56 was an unmanned, planned-loss device made of wood with a load of 1,000 kg of fuel, which could be connected to a fighter aircraft by ropes and a fuel line in the lift tow. This enabled the range of a Focke Wulf Fw 190 to be doubled from 800 to up to 1,600 km. Using the same principle, it was possible to carry additional bombloads to targets. For example, a 1,000-kg bomb was fitted with dropping wings, enlarged tail assemblies, and similar to the fuel carrier, was pulled behind tow planes. This enabled the Fw 190, for example, to fully exploit its capabilities as a fighter plane after the bomb was released. The bomb carrier received the project title Gotha P-57. As the P-58, GWF finally proposed a cannon-armed manned glider, which could then be brought to the target by the tow plane for a single attack flight. However, these suggestions remained stuck in the project status.

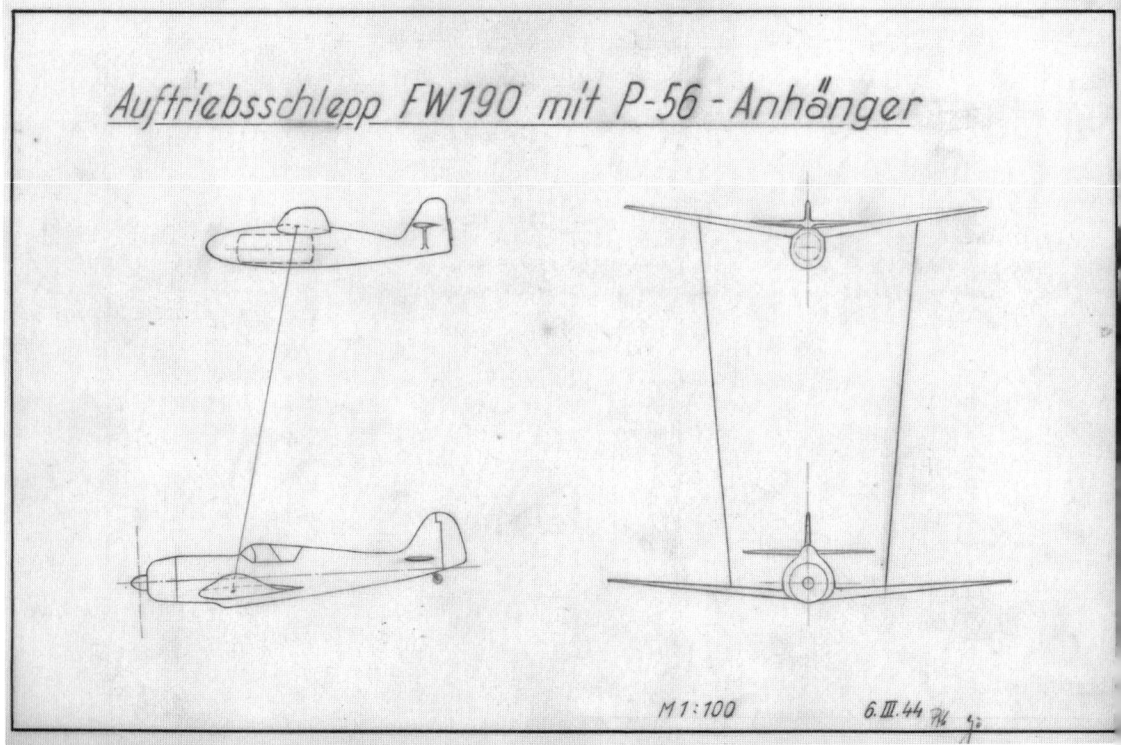

Fw 190 with P-56 trailer. (*DEHLA*)

Dr Rudolf Göthert

The aerodynamicist Rudolf Göthert, born in Hanover in 1912, studied physics and mathematics at the technical university in his hometown. His older brother Bernhard Göthert got him a job in 1935 at the wind tunnel of the Technical University in Braunschweig, where he also wrote his doctoral thesis. In 1937, he became head of the low-speed wind tunnel at the Institute for Aerodynamics at the Aviation Research Institute in Braunschweig. In 1942, Rudolf Göthert moved to the design office of Gotha Wagon Factory as an aerodynamicist and did research on the new lift tow method for cargo gliders. Among other things, he was also involved in the construction of the Go 345 cargo glider. Commencing in 1944, Göthert belonged to the elevator and rudder section of the advisory board of the special committee for wind tunnels, which advised the German aviation industry on aerodynamic issues. His brother Bernhard was also a member of this advisory board and was responsible for general high-speed issues. Rudolf Göthert quickly recognised the aerodynamic weaknesses of the Horten 229, which GWF was to produce in series and designed his own flying wing, the Gotha P-60. After the war

Rudolf Göthert
(1912–1973).
(*Manfred Göthert*)

ended, the Americans were interested in his knowledge, and that of other German high-tech specialists. He received an offer from the French to contribute his skills to the French aviation industry. Göthert was given a five-year contract and was involved in the development of a family of flying wing jets at the Société Nationale de Constructions Aéronautiques du Sud-Est (SNCASE) in Marignane in southern France. However, the elaborate, futuristic designs, including a flying wing airliner with six jet engines, quickly disappeared into storage. Rudolf Göthert returned early to Germany and in 1947 was once again the head of the wind tunnel in Braunschweig. He died of a heart attack in 1973.

Gotha P-60 A, P-60 B, P-60 C—Fighter Aircraft, Fighter-Bomber, Night Fighter

The many problems and delays in the series-ready redesign of the flying wing Horten Ho 229 prompted GWF at the end of 1944 to design its own aircraft in this style. An additional factor was that the RLM had reduced its original order of 100 Ho 229 series aircraft to just 20 aircraft. Also, with an in-house design, there was a great opportunity to be able to produce their own aircraft in series again after the Go 242 contract expired. Based on the experiences with the Horton flying wing and at the request of the *Oberkommando der Luftwaffe* (OKL—High Command of the Air Force), Dr Rudolf Göthert, together with his assistant graduate engineer Hans Neuber, built an independent flying wing jet aircraft. The OKL had asked for a high-speed aircraft with a crew of two, a pressure-tight altitude chamber, nose landing gear and the possibility of installing more powerful engines, which could be used for fighter, bombing, and exploration at close and medium distances. On 8 January 1945, GWF presented the Gotha P-60 project to the head of technical air armament, in which not only the wishes of the OKL but also the latest findings in high-speed research from the special committee for wind tunnels were incorporated. Rudolf Göthert and his brother Bernhard belonged to this group. A tubular steel frame was planned for the flying wing Gotha P-60, which was covered with plywood and consisted of the two outer wings and the middle wing in which the crew compartment was located. It was completely housed within the normal profile. The two-man crew, consisting of the pilot and radio operator lay staggered in relation to one another in the crew room at the tip of the centre wing. The crew was protected against fire from the front and the side by armoured cradles and 100-mm-thick bulletproof glass panes.

The armament, radio, and most of the equipment, along with the retractable landing gear were located in the central wing, which could be walked along in its entirety. The outer wings also consisted of a tubular steel frame covered with wood. The fuel tanks were housed in the hollows of the wings.

Two internally balanced rudders on the trailing edge of the wings were responsible for the aircraft's elevation and aileron controls. The rudder control was to be achieved by two symmetrically extendable, up and down, control surfaces near the wing tips. Two BMW 003 jet engines were planned as the propulsion system, arranged symmetrically above and below the centre wing. As a variant, a twin arrangement was still being considered, in which the two engines were to be sunk below the centre wing. In order to check the appropriateness of this engine arrangement, the GWF had wind tunnel investigations carried out.

For the chassis, the designers used the model used in the Junkers Ju 88 A-4. Either four 30-mm MK 108 automatic cannons with a total of 670 rounds or two MK 103 with a total of 350 rounds were planned as armament. The basic design was named Gotha P-60 A.[28] The aircraft was revised again by Göthert and Neuber when the OKL required a further developed design that was to have an increased range and expanded installation space inside the fuselage for more extensive equipment. In addition, instead of the BMW 003, two jet engines of the 109.011 power class (Heinkel HeS 011 jet engines with 12.7 kN thrust each) were required. The slightly enlarged version of the flying wing was given the name Gotha P-60 B. At the same time, GWF presented a draft for a night fighter variant, the Gotha P-60 C to the OKL on 11 March. Compared to the P-60 B, the installation of the FuG 240 radar in the bow required an additional front structure on the centre wing. Behind this additional bow, the pilot and radio operator sat behind one another in a pressure-tight cockpit under a teardrop-shaped viewing hood. The viewing hood could be thrown off so that the crew could use the ejection seat to rescue themselves in an emergency. For reasons of stability caused by the additional bow, it was necessary to install conventional vertical stabilisers, which were located on the rear edge of the outer wings. Otherwise, the design was similar to that of the P-60 B. Two Heinkel HeS 011 engines were also planned.[29] In addition to the forward-facing four 30-mm MK 108 cannons, an angled armament '*schräge Musik*' of two to four automatic MK 108 or MK 213 was possible as a conversion kit in the centre wing. The first wind tunnel tests of models of the Gotha P-60 started in Göttingen and at the German Aviation Research Institute (DVL) in Berlin. Further wind tunnel models were in the works. In the summer of 1945, the first test flights were to take place at the E-Stelle in Rechlin. However, due to the end of the war, no dummy models or prototypes were built. The HeS 011, at that time the world's most powerful jet engine, was still under development. If a prototype had actually been built, the superiority of the GWF project over the Ho 229 would have been shown very quickly.

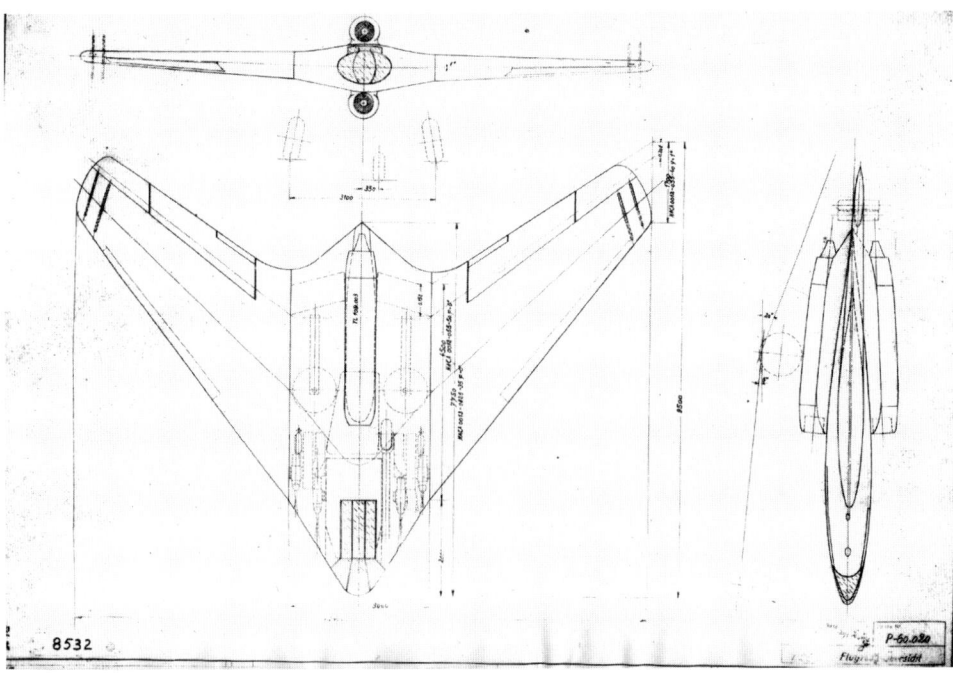

Project drawing of the Gotha P-60A, two jet engines—BMW 003 were arranged symmetrically to each other above and below the centre wing. (*Manfred Göthert*)

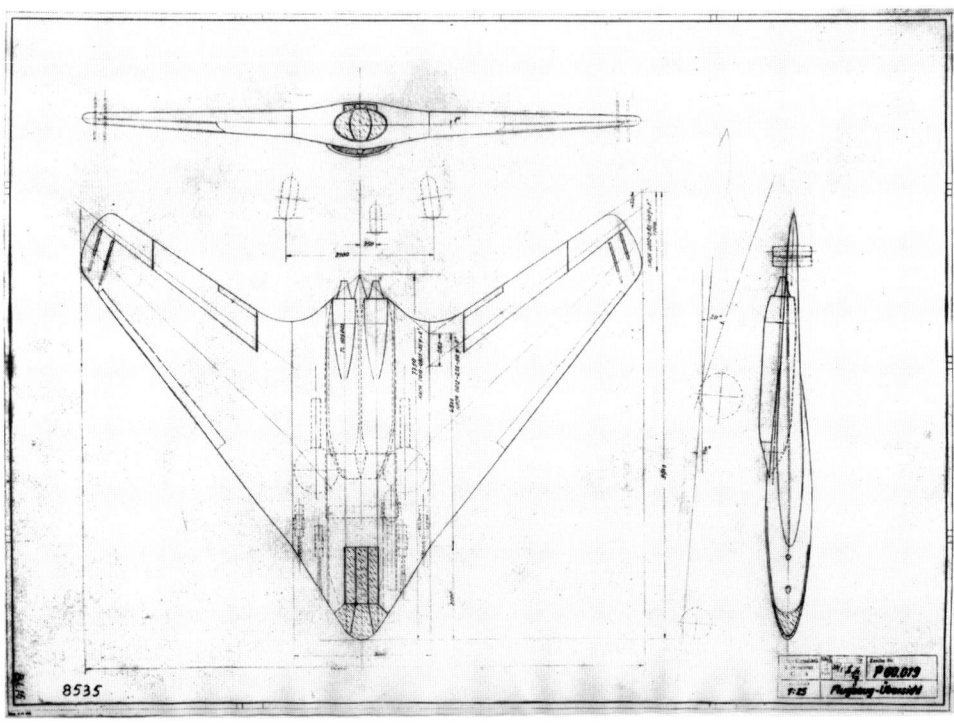

As a variant, a twin arrangement of the two engines below the centre wing of the P-60 was planned. (*Manfred Göthert*)

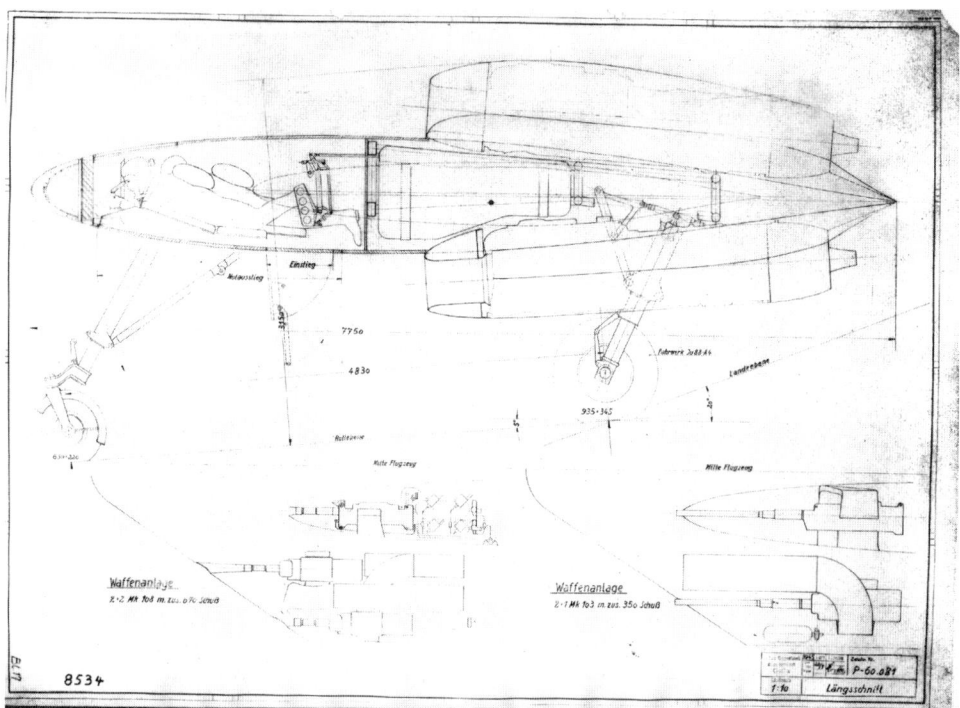

Longitudinal section through the P-60: The two-man crew consisting of the pilot and radio operator lay staggered in relation to each other in the crew compartment at the tip of the centre wing. (*Manfred Göthert*)

This is how the Gotha P-60 C, the night-fighter variant of the flying wing would have looked. This replica is in the aeronautical museum in Rechlin. (*Luftfahrttechnisches Museum Rechlin*)

11

1945–1953:
ALLIED OCCUPATION, DISMANTLING AND RECONSTRUCTION

When the city of Gotha was occupied by American troops on 4 April 1945, aircraft production at the Gotha Wagon Factory ended. The day before, the company had laid off 1,400 employees. About 300 employees remained in Gotha and 110 in Ilmenau, who from then on only managed the remnants of the destroyed production facilities. As decided at the Yalta conference in February 1945 between the USA, Great Britain, and the Soviet Union, the state of Thuringia and thus the cities of Gotha and Ilmenau had been added to the Soviet zone of occupation. Starting on 1 July 1945 the occupation change was to take place. The Americans therefore lost no time in the search for the latest military technology and German scientists. One day, after the Ho-229 prototype had been found in Friedrichroda along with the design documents for the Gotha P-60, two Americans stood at the doorstep of GWF aerodynamicist Rudolf Göthert. Before they took him to Paris, Göthert convinced them to promise to bring his wife and son to safety. The management of GWF also withdrew to the West well before the Soviet occupation troops marched in.

On 1 July 1945, as agreed, Soviet troops replaced the Americans in Thuringia. On behalf of the new occupying power, the city of Gotha prepared a status report regarding the situation of Gotha Wagon Factory. According to the report, the Reich still owed the company 40 million Reichsmarks, which were offset by liabilities of various banks in the amount of 28 million Reichsmarks. Payments from the Reich were no longer to be expected, there were no new revenues, the directors had disappeared, and the question of ownership was unclear—the end of GWF was only a matter of time. As if that was not enough, the Soviet military government confiscated the former armaments factory on 29 August 1945 and began to systematically dismantle it. All of the material that was still available, including those from the subsidiaries, became spoils of war. Three aircraft construction halls, 62, 63, and 65, parts of which were already being rebuilt, were dismantled by the

The end: An American B-24 flies over the ruins of GWF on 11 May 1945. (*USAF*)

Soviet occupiers and transported away, along with all the technical equipment. The remaining halls which had been damaged by the bombing were demolished and the runways of the airfield were blown up. The numerous aircraft wrecks on the site ended up as scrap metal. The Soviets also had the air base, in which part of the aircraft production had been relocated during the war, completely levelled except for the residential buildings of the barracks. In addition to aircraft construction, which was completely eliminated, it also affected the area of wagon construction. Here, too, machines and equipment were transported to the Soviet Union as spoils of war. While the dismantlement was taking place, simple consumer goods such as briefcases, horseshoes, farm wagons, handcarts, and toboggans were manufactured in this area. In addition, GWF also carried out saddlery and carpentry work for the Soviet military. Starting at the end of 1945, the repair of railway wagons and trams began again, and new ones were soon produced.[30] On 18 July 1948, by decision of the Thuringian state government and by order of the Soviet occupying power, Gotha Wagon Factory became public property.[31] The company was thus nationalised as *Volkseigener Betrieb Waggonbau Gotha* (VEB—publicly owned Wagon Construction Company Gotha). This ensured the company's continued existence for the time being in Gotha. Business was slowly improving again, but in contrast, the branch in Ilmenau closed in 1951. The Gotha-Ilmenauer Flugzeugbau GmbH was expropriated on 17 April 1948 and transferred to public ownership. Up until then, the plant had carried out orders for the occupiers, repaired damaged wagons, and manufactured handcarts and other consumer goods for the population. There had been no connection to the parent company after the Soviet occupation forces set up their own management. At the request of the Thuringian Ministry of the Interior, the company, which had meanwhile been run as having 'no assets', was deleted from the commercial register on 7 May 1951.[32]

12

1953–1954:
Gliders for the GDR

In 1945, aircraft construction in Germany was banned by the victorious powers. In the early 1950s, the rumour arose in the Soviet occupation zone that these restrictions would be relaxed. Some war returnees and former aircraft builders of GWF also heard the rumours and decided to resume their pre-war hobby and work from home to recreate two SG 38 training gliders. When the GDR authorities found out about the replicas, they confiscated the two unfinished gliders. Returned in 1952 and completed, the aircraft soon became part of the Gotha branch of the *Gesellschaft für Sport und Technik* (GST—Sport and Technology Association). These illegal replicas may have been the impetus to revive aircraft construction in Gotha for a short time. At the end of the day, the GST desperately needed aircraft for glider training. The pre-military organisation founded in 1952 was the only legal possibility in the GDR to operate glider or motorised flight. As in the Third Reich, pilots often ended up at the controls of a military aircraft.

Schulgleiter SG 38—Glider

In 1953, the GDR authorities commissioned VEB Waggonbau Gotha to replicate the pre-war SG 38 and Grunau Baby IIb gliders for the GST. The training glider SG 38 was an open, single-seat glider made of wooden profiles for beginners' training. The relatively easy to manufacture, open cockpit beginner glider, was produced by the thousands. Not only by the industry, but also in many clubs according to open source plans dating from the end of the 1930s. An unknown number of SG 38 and Grunau Baby aircraft were created for the local NSFK (*Nationalsozialistisches Fliegerkorps*) group. These aircraft were also produced in the training workshop of GWF. However, no sooner had post-war production of the SG 38 started in Gotha than the factory management had to ask the public

Post-war production: 329 units of the SG 38 training glider were built in Gotha. (*Dlugosch collection*)

This SG 38, built in 1954 Gotha, was restored in Bad Berka in 2018. (*Author's collection*)

for support: there was a shortage of shock absorbers to be built into the runners of the gliders. Since there was no other way to help at first, three interconnected rubber buffers were installed. However, the cushioning during landing was insufficient, and the runners often broke. It is not known if or how many shock absorbers were actually donated after the call. Production of the SG 38 in Gotha ended in 1954 after a total of 330 units and 200 kits had been delivered.

Grunau Baby IIb—Glider

The training and exercise glider Grunau Baby IIb was designed in 1932 for beginners' training. The single-seat glider was a braced, high-wing glider made of wood. Compared to the previous Baby II and Baby IIa models, the Baby IIb version built in Gotha had a trapezoidal wing layout. Up until the final cessation of aircraft production in Gotha, 104 aircraft had been built there. That was only a small fraction of the more than 4,000 Baby I, Baby IIa, and Baby IIb that were built around the world by the 1950s. This makes the aircraft one of the most common gliders in the world after the SG 38.

Grunau Baby IIb at Gotha Airfield: From 1953 to 1954, VEB Waggonbau Gotha built a total of 104 units of the single-seat glider. (*Dlugosch collection*)

Gotha Go 530 (FES 530 Lehrmeister)—Training Glider

In addition to the production of SG 38 and Baby IIb, the GDR government commissioned VEB Waggonbau Gotha to construct a two-seater training and exercise glider in wood construction for beginner, performance, and thermal training. With the two-seater, the single-seat and open SG 38 was to be replaced in glider training. In the winter of 1953, a final, independent construction was built in Gotha. The designer Hans Hartung, together with the aerodynamicist Hans Wegerich and the structural engineer Wilhelm Zimmermann, designed a two-seater, braced high-wing aircraft with two seats arranged one behind the other. The maiden flight of the first test model, the Go 530 V-1, took place on 15 June 1954 at the nearby airfield in Bienstädt, as the old GWF factory airfield, which had been blown up, was not yet usable. The pilot was the head of glider production, Gerhard Renner. The first flight was successful, but the prototype broke on one of the following flights. After that, Renner's permission for further test flights was withdrawn. He later moved to West Germany. The further flight tests of the repaired V-1 and the now completed second test model, the Go 530 V-2, then took place in Laucha and Kamenz. Before production could start at VEB Waggonbau Gotha, the SED leadership decided to relocate GDR glider production to Lommatzsch, north of Dresden, commencing on 1 March 1955. The new glider was officially approved in November 1955, but a few deficiencies had to be corrected before series production. With the relocation to Lommatzsch, aircraft construction at Gotha came to a final end. Referred to as the FES 530 *Lehrmeister* (Instructor) (FES—research and development centre), the Go 530 went into series production in 1957. After a total of 100 FES 530 Lehrmeisters had been built, production was switched to the improved version, the FES 530 Lehrmeister I. The wing was now cantilevered, but the wing spar and the main bulkhead were redesigned again. The result was a weight saving of 20 kg compared to the previous model and simplified handling during assembly and disassembly of the aircraft. A total 22 units of this variant were produced. The FES 530 Lehrmeister II followed with a span that was reduced from 17 to 15 metres. A total of 223 FES 530s, including the two prototypes, were built and mainly used for glider training in the GST. Some gliders were exported to Egypt, Denmark, Syria, and other countries. The last machine designed in Gotha was the first GDR aircraft to be mass-produced after the end of the war.

Above and below: First flight of the training glider Go 530 V1 on 15 June 1954 at the Bienstädt airfield, near Gotha. (*Horst Kunisch*)

Before take-off: FES 530 II, a further development of the Go 530, shortly before take-off from Gotha airfield, sometime in the mid-1960s. (*Horst Kunisch*)

The 'fathers' of the Go 530/FES 530: The aerodynamics engineer Hans Wegerich, the designer Hans Hartung, and the structural engineer Wilhelm Zimmermann. (*Krieg collection*)

13

1954–2017:
SOCIALIST PLANNED ECONOMY AND REPRIVATISATION

After the relocation of aircraft production to Lommatzsch, and the three Go/FES 530 designers also moved to Saxony, VEB Waggonbau Gotha concentrated on building trams and freight wagons. Commencing in 1967, the company's production profile changed. The construction of rail vehicles was completely stopped. The renamed company, VEB Luft- und Kältetechnik Gotha, now built fans and cooling systems. In 1983, vehicle construction was resumed. The company, which had since been run under the name VEB Kraftfahrzeugwerk Gotha (Motor Vehicle Plant Gotha), now manufactured chassis for Wartburg cars and was a supplier to the automobile plant in Eisenach. Some 60 years earlier, the Eisenach company had been a subsidiary of GWF before it was sold to BMW in 1928. In March 1990, following a resolution by the last GDR government, the *Treuhandgesellschaft* (trust company) took over the administration of all GDR state-owned companies in order to privatise them. The former VEB Kraftfahrzeugwerk Gotha also got new owners. The company was split up. One part became a subsidiary of Schmitz Cargobull, a manufacturer of semi-trailers and truck trailers, since 1997. The other part, Gothaer Fahrzeugtechnik GmbH, has specialised in the construction of lattice masts for crane booms. In 2013, Gothaer Fahrzeugtechnik briefly returned to aircraft construction. For a reconstruction project, the company rebuilt the lattice fuselage of a Gotha Go 145. Some of the old GWF airfield in Gotha-Ost still exists today. In the late 1950s, GST flight students built a new base from the rubble of the destroyed GWF and reactivated part of the old runway. For many years, they were present in the sky over Gotha with their gliders. In 1979, many airfields close to the border with West Germany came to an end due to financial reasons. The Gotha airfield was also closed. After 1990, the old aviators got together again, founded the *Flugsportverein Gotha* (Aviation club Gotha) and restored the old airfield. It is still in operation today.

In August 2013, Gothaer Fahrzeugtechnik completed the replica of the lattice fuselage of a Go 145. Next to it is the original fuselage. (*Author's collection*)

After the end of the GDR, two companies settled on the site of the former Gothaer wagon factory (above the railway line), the trailer manufacturer Schmitz Cargobull and Gothaer Fahrzeugtechnik, a manufacturer of lattice masts for crane booms. The V-contour of the former GWF airfield can still be seen clearly. (*Author's collection*)

Epilogue and Acknowledgements

In this book, it was important to me not only to introduce the many different types of aircraft that were built in Gotha, with some interruptions, between 1913 and 1954, but also to tell the eventful history of Gotha Wagon Factory dominated by its rise and fall. This especially rings true for the aircraft construction department. After the climax of both wars, a catastrophic crash followed with the temporary end of aircraft construction. This was largely due to the fact that with very few exceptions, only military aircraft were built in Gotha. Inextricably linked to the history of the company were the fates of the designers and pilots who were witnesses to these moments in history. The human factor was, therefore, my driving force during the research for this book. However, different sources with partially contradicting information have not made it easy to evaluate facts and may have led to incorrect conclusions and errors. I would therefore be grateful for any information or additions. Contact: ASP.Metzmacher@gmail.com

I am also very grateful to the many supporters of this project. First and foremost is Marton Szigeti, from Düsseldorf, who not only provided me with numerous documents and photographs, but also technical support for the manuscript. Without his intensive, time-consuming supervision, it would not have been possible to complete this book on this scale.

Important support came from my colleague Michael Wenkel, from Erfurt, who, as the 'first reader' of the manuscript, made sure that it would accessible to the general reader and not just aircraft technicians. I would like to thank Jörg Mückler, from Berlin, for the final technical and editorial fine-tuning; Manfred Krieg, from Erfurt; Dr Volker Koos, from Rostock; Mirko Schinnerling, from Dresden; and Peter Dlugosch, from Gotha, for providing me with information and photographs. I thank also Manfred Göthert, from Hamburg, for the original project documents from his father. Finally, I would like to thank my wife, Susanne, who always supported me, even when I spent my evenings with the book and our family life suffered.

Andreas Metzmacher
December 2020

Appendix: General Characteristics Gotha Aircraft

Type	Usage	Powerplant	Wingspan (m)	Length (m)	Height (m)	Empty weight (kg)	Maximum speed (kph)	Range (km)	Armament	Crew
LE 1	Training aircraft	1 × Mercedes D I, 75 HP	14.45	7.8	-	570	90	-	-	2
LE 2	Training, reconnaissance aircraft	1 × Mercedes D I, 100 HP	14.45	10.3	3.2	600	92	-	-	2
LE 3	Training, reconnaissance aircraft	1 × Mercedes D I, 100 HP	14.5	10.0	3.15	690	96	385	-	2
LE 4	Training aircraft	1 × Mercedes D I, 100 HP	14.0	8.5	-	610	120	-	-	2
LD 1	Training, reconnaissance aircraft	1 × Oberursel U 1, 100 HP	12.55	8.3	3.25	525	115	520	-	2
LD 2	Reconnaissance aircraft	1 × Mercedes D I, 100 HP	14.5	8.4	3.45	735	120	450	-	2
LD 3	Training aircraft	1 × Gnome 7 Omega, 50 HP	13.28	6.85	-	445	110	-	-	2
LD 4	Training aircraft	1 × Gnome 9 Delta, 100 HP	13.28	6.85	-	-	-	-	-	2
LD 5	Training, reconnaissance aircraft	1 × Oberursel U 1, 100 HP	8.5	-	-	-	-	-	-	1
LD 6	Training, reconnaissance aircraft	1 × Benz II, 150 HP	-	-	-	-	-	-	-	2
LD 7	Training, reconnaissance aircraft	1 × Mercedes D II, 120 HP	12.4	8.4	3	725	125	530	-	2
G I	Armed escort aircraft, bomber	2 × Benz Bz III, 160 HP	20.3	12.1	3.9	1800	130	540	1 × 7.92 mm MG 14 150 kg bombs	3
G II	Bomber	2 × Mercedes D IV, 220 HP	23.7	12.42	4.3	2180	148	700	2 × 7.92 mm MG 14 450 kg bombs	3
G III	Bomber	2 × Mercedes D IVa, 260 HP	23.7	12.42	4.3	2193	140	-	3 × 7.92 mm MG 14 500 kg bombs	3
G IV	Bomber	2 × Mercedes D IVa, 260 HP	23.7	12.42	4.3	2400	140	490	3 × 7.92 mm MG 14 500 kg bombs	3
G V	Bomber	2 × Mercedes D IVa, 260 HP	23.7	12.42	4.3	2570	140	840	3 × 7.92 mm MG 14 500 kg bombs	3
G Va	Bomber	2 × Mercedes D IVa, 260 HP	23.7	12.42	4.3	2740	140	840	3 × 7.92 mm MG 14 600 kg bombs	3
G Vb	Bomber	2 × Mercedes D IVa, 260 HP	23.7	12.42	4.3	2950	135	810	3 × 7.92 mm MG 14 600 kg bombs	3
G VI	Experimental aircraft	2 × Mercedes D IVa, 260 HP	21.5	12.42	-	-	-	-	-	3
G VII	Reconnaissance aircraft, bomber	2 × Mercedes D IVa, 260 HP	19.27	9.63	3.5	2420	180	540	1 × 7.92 mm MG 14 without specification bombs	2
G VIII	Bomber	2 × Maybach Mb IVa, 240 HP	21.73	9.79	3.5	2676	180	500	2 × 7.92 mm MG 14	2
G IX	Bomber	2 × Maybach Mb IVa, 240 HP	25.26	9.79	-	-	-	-	2 × 7.92 mm MG 14 250 kg bombs	2
GL X	Reconnaissance, attack aircraft	2 × BMW IIIa, 185 HP	-	-	-	-	-	-	-	2
WD 1a	Sea reconnaissance aircraft	1 × Mercedes D I, 100 HP	14.1	10.3	4	800	90	540	-	2

Type	Usage	Powerplant	Wingspan (m)	Length (m)	Height (m)	Empty weight (kg)	Maximum speed (kph)	Range (km)	Armament	Crew
WD 2	Sea reconnaissance aircraft	1 × Benz Bz III, 150 HP	15.6	10.5	4.1	1065	112	670	1 × 7.92 mm MG 14	2
WD 3	Sea reconnaissance aircraft	1 × Mercedes D III, 160 HP	15.6			1185	100		1 × 7.92 mm MG	3
UWD	Sea reconnaissance aircraft, bomber	2 × Mercedes D III, 160 HP	20.1	14.2	4.4	1940	128	480	1 × 7.92 mm MG 14 300 kg bombs	2
WD 5	Sea reconnaissance aircraft	1 × Mercedes D III, 160 HP	12.5	10.3	3.8	980	126	440	without specification bombs	2
WD 7	Sea reconnaissance aircraft, bomber	2 × Mercedes D II, 120 HP	16	11.3	3.9	1440	136	475	1 × 7.92 mm MG 14 without specification bombs	2
WD 8	Sea reconnaissance aircraft	1 × Maybach MB IVa, 240 HP	16	11.2	4.1	1254	135	480	1 × 7.92 mm MG 14 without specification. bombs	2
WD 9	Sea reconnaissance aircraft	1 × Mercedes D III, 160 HP	12.5	-	-	968	132	-	1 × 7.92 mm MG 14	2
WD 11	Torpedo aircraft	2 × Mercedes D III, 160 HP	22.5	13.5	4.8	2175	120	500	1 × 7.92 mm MG 14 1 torpedo	2
WD 12	Sea reconnaissance aircraft	1 × Mercedes D III, 160 HP	15	10	3.8	1000	141	770	-	2
WD 13	Training, sea reconnaissance aircraft	1 × Benz Bz III, 150 HP	15.1	10	3.74	1970	132	130	1 × 7.92 mm MG 14	2
WD 14	Torpedo, sea reconnaissance aircraft	2 × Benz Bz IV, 200 HP	25	14.5	5	2875	130	780	2 × 7.92 mm MG 14 1 torpedo	2
WD 15	Sea reconnaissance aircraft	1 × Mercedes D IVa, 260 HP	17.2	11.2	4.3	1545	152	900	-	2
WD 20	Sea reconnaissance aircraft	2 × Mercedes D IVa, 260 HP	26	14.4	5	3030	126		2 × 7.92 mm MG 14 1 torpedo	2
WD 22	Sea reconnaissance aircraft	2 × Mercedes D III, 160 HP 2 × Mercedes D I, 100 HP	26	14.4	5.2	3800	131	750	2 × 7.92 mm MG 14	2
WD 27	Sea reconnaissance aircraft	4 × Mercedes D IIIa, 175 HP	34	17.6	6	4500	141	810	2 × 7.92 mm MG 14	2
WD 28	Reconnaissance aircraft	1 × Mercedes D IVa, 260 HP	17.5	11.3	4.3	1480	140	770	-	2
Go 145 A	Training aircraft	1 × Argus As 10 C, 240 HP	9.0	8.7	2.9	880	212	630	-	2
Go 146	Touring aircraft	2 × Hirth HM 508E, 280 HP	11.5	9	2.85	1400	335	1000	-	1 + 4
Go 147	Experimental aircraft	1 × Argus As 10 C, 240 HP	11.0	6.7	2.54	945	220	420	1 × 7.92 mm MG 15	2
Go 149	Training aircraft	1 × Argus As 10 C, 240 HP	7.8	7.3	2.1	800	345	800	-	1
Go 150	Touring aircraft	2 × Zündapp Z 9-092, 50 HP	11.8	7.15	2,03	512	200	900	-	2
Go 241	Touring aircraft	2 × Hirth HM 506 A, 160 HP	14.5	9.02	2.52	1370	275	800	-	2
Go 242 A-1	Cargo glider	-	24.5	15.8	4.4	3236	240	-	3 × 7.92 mm MG 15	1 + 3
Go 244 B-2	Transport aircraft	2 × Gnome-Rhône 14M, 740 HP	24.5	15.8	4.7	5224	290	480	3 × 7.92 mm MG 15	2 + 27
Go 345 B	Cargo glider	-	21.0	13.0	4.2	2395	310	-	-	2 + 10
Go 530 (FES 530)	Training glider	-	17.0	7.95	2.12	300	200	-	-	2

General Characteristics Aircraft Produced Under License

Type	Usage	Powerplant	Wingspan (m)	Length (m)	Height (m)	Empty Weight (kg)	Maximum speed (kph)	Range (km)	Armament	Crew
Willing Eindecker	Training aircraft	1 × Rheinische Aerowerke Düsseldorf, 50/60 HP	-	-	-	-	-	-	-	1
Büchner Doppeldecker	Training aircraft	1 × Argus As I, 70 HP	20.0	10.5	-	-	-	-	-	2
Büchner Wasserdoppeldecker	Competition aircraft	1 × Mercedes D I, 100 HP	20.0	10.4	-	750	-	-	-	1
Hansa-Brandenburg NW (Gotha WD 6)	Sea reconnaissance aircraft	1 × Mercedes D III, 160 HP	16.27	9.85	3.75	1052	121	600	50 kg bombs	2
Friedrichshafen FF 49c	Sea reconnaissance aircraft	1 × Benz Bz IV, 240 HP	17.15	11.65	4.5	1515	140	700	2 × 7.92 mm MG 14	2
Friedrichshafen G Iva	Bomber	2 × Mercedes D IVa, 260 HP	22.6	12.0	3.5	2897	142	600	2 × 7.92 mm MG 14 1000 kg bombs	3
Heinkel He 45c	Reconnaissance aircraft, light bomber	1 × BMW VI, 600 HP	11.5	10.6	3.6	2110	290	1200	1 × 7.92-mm MG 17 1 × 7.92-mm MG 15	2
Heinkel He 46 D	Reconnaissance aircraft	1 × SAM 22B, 600 HP	14.0	9.5	3.4	1765	250	1000	-	2
Focke Wulf Fw 58 C-2	Training. liaison aircraft	2 × Argus As 10 C, 240 HP	21.05	14	4.5	1960	265	1080	-	4
Deutsche Forschungsanstalt für Segelflug DFS 230 A-2	Cargo glider	-	21.98	11.24	2.74	860	215	-	1 × 7.92 mm MG 34	1 + 9
Deutsche Forschungsanstalt für Segelflug DFS 331	Cargo glider	-	23.0	15.81	3.55	2270	270	-	-	1 + 18
Messerschmitt Bf 110 B-1	Heavy fighter	2 × Jumo 210 G, 730 HP	16.9	12.07	3.9	5650	480	1200	1 × 7.92 mm MG 15 4 × 7.92 mm MG 17 2 × 20 mm MG FF	2
Messerschmitt Bf 110 C-1	Heavy fighter, fighter bomber	2 × Daimler-Benz DB 601 A, 1000 HP	16.28	12.07	4.1	5150	530	800	1 × 7.92 mm MG 15 4 × 7.92 mm MG 17 2 × 20 mm MG FF	2
Messerschmitt Bf 110 F-2	Heavy fighter, fighter bomber	2 × Daimler-Benz DB 601 F, 1350 HP	16.28	12.07	4	5600	570	1200	1 × 7.92 mm MG 81Z 4 × 7.92 mm MG 17 2 × 20 mm MG FF/M	2
Messerschmitt Bf 110 G-4	Night fighter	2 × Daimler-Benz DB 605 B, 1475 HP	16.29	12.68	3.98	6090	510	880	4 × 7.92 mm MG 17 2 × 20-mm MG 151/20 1 × 7.92 mm MG 81Z	3

Type	Usage	Powerplant	Wingspan (m)	Length (m)	Height (m)	Empty Weight (kg)	Maximum speed (kph)	Range (km)	Armament	Crew
Messerschmitt Me 210 A-1	Heavy fighter, fighter bomber	2 × Daimler-Benz DB 601 F, 1350 HP	16.4	12.15	3.7	9690	573	1820	2 × 7.92 mm MG 17 2 × 20 mm MG 151/20 2 × MG 131 1000 kg bombs	2
Focke-Wulf Ta 152 H-1	High-altitude fighter	Junkers Jumo 213 E-1, 1750 HP	14.82	10.82	3.36	3920	730	1200	1 × 30 mm MK 108 2 × 20 mm MG151/20	1
Horten Ho 229	Fighter	2 × Junkers Jumo 004B, 8.7 kN	16.76	7.47	2.81	4600	970	1900	4 × 30 mm MK 108	1
Schulgleiter SG 38	Glider	-	10.42	6.28	2.43	125	115	-	-	1
Grunau Baby IIb	Glider	-	13.5	6.15	1.35	160	160	-	-	1

Abbreviations

AEG	Allgemeine Elektrizitäts-Gesellschaft AG	GWF	Gothaer Waggonfabrik AG
		Idflieg	Inspektion der Fliegertruppen
As	Argus	Jumo	Junkers Motor
BFW	Bayerische Flugzeugwerke AG	Kagohl	Kampfgeschwader der Obersten Heeresleitung
BMW	Bayerische Motorenwerke AG		
Bogohl	Bombengeschwader der Obersten Heeresleitung	LD	Landdoppeldecker
		LE	Landeindecker
Bz	Benz	LVG	Luftverkehrsgesellschaft mbH
D	Daimler (Mercedes-Motor)	Mb	Maybach
DMG	Daimler Motorengesellschaft	NSFK	Nationalsozialistisches Fliegerkorps
DDR	Deutsche Demokratische Republik		
		OKL	Oberkommando der Luftwaffe
DFS	Deutsche Forschungsanstalt für Segelflug	R	Riesenflugzeug
		RAF	Royal Air Force
DLV	Deutscher Luftsportverband	RFA	Riesen-Flugzeug-Abteilung
d.R.	der Reserve	RKL	Reichskommissariat für Luftfahrt
FAI	Fédération Aèronautique Internationale	RLM	Reichsluftfahrtministerium
		RMA	Reichsmarineamt
FEA	Fliegerersatz-Abteilung	SED	Sozialistische Einheitspartei Deutschlands
FES	Forschungs- und Entwicklungsstelle		
		SG	Schulgleiter
FF	Flugzeugbau Friedrichshafen GmbH	SNCASE	Société Nationale de Constructions Aéronautiques du Sud-Est
FFA	Feldflieger-Abteilung		
FU	Friedel-Ursinus	SSW	Siemens-Schuckert Werke GmbH
Fw	Focke-Wulf	SVK	Seeflugzeug-Versuchskommando
G	Großflugzeug	USAAF	United States Army Air Force
GDR	German Democratic Republic	USAF	United States Air Force
GIF	Gotha-Ilmenauer Flugzeugbau GmbH	UWD	Ursinus-Wasserdoppeldecker
		VEB	Volkseigener Betrieb
GmbH	Gesellschaft mit beschränkter Haftung	VGO	Versuchsbau Gotha-Ost
		WD	Wasserdoppeldecker
GST	Gesellschaft für Sport und Technik		

Bibliography

Bowers, Peter M., 'The Gotha Bombers', *American Modeler*, 1960.
Flugsport—illustrierte flugtechnische Zeitschrift für das gesamte Flug-Wesen, Nr. 13/1919
  'Gothaer Waggonfabrik', *Der Flieger*, 02/1942.
Gotha Go 145, Go 146, Go 149 und Go 150—Werksprospekte der Gothaer Waggonfabrik, Luftfahrt Archiv Hafner.
Grosz, Peter M., 'Gotha Aircraft', unveröffentlichtes Manuskript 2002'.
Grosz, Peter M., Nachlass im Deutschen Technikmuseum Berlin.
Haddow, G. W.; Grosz, Peter M., *The German Giants*' Putnam & Company Limited London, 1962. Israel, Ulrich 'Deutsche Torpedobomber im Ersten Weltkrieg', *Flieger Revue Extra*, Heft 25, 2009.
Kens, Karlheinz, 'Gotha Go 147—Experimente für einen Nahaufklärer' *Modellflug International* 8/2008.
Mankau, Heinz; Petrick, Peter, *Messerschmitt Bf 110, Me 210, Me 410*, Aviatic Verlag, 2001.
Mankau, Heinz; Petrick, Peter, *Deutsche Lastensegler*, Motorbuch Verlag, 2008.
Lemke, Frank-Dieter, *Segelflugzeugbau in der DDR*, Verlag Rockstuhl, 2018.
'Männer der deutschen Luftfahrt—Bruno Büchner', *Der Flieger*, 4/1944.
'Männer der deutschen Luftfahrt – Karl F. M. Rösner', *Der Flieger*, 10/1942.
Metzmacher, Andreas, 'One for the record', *Aeroplane Monthly*, 10/2009.
Mückler, Jörg, *Deutsche Bomber im Ersten Weltkrieg*, Motorbuch Verlag Stuttgart, 2017.
Norman, Bill, 'Me 210 Intruder Raid' *FlyPast*, 9/2010.
Nowarra, Heinz Joachim, *Die deutsche Luftrüstung 1933–1945*, Bernard & Graefe Verlag 1993.
Pawlas, Karl R., *Luftfahrt International 1, Luftfahrt-Lexikon Fw 58 Weihe*.
Roschmann, Winfried; Sponsel, Udo; Jesussek, Bernd, *Die Fürther Hardhöhe* Städtebilder-Verlag Fürth, 1999.
Szigeti, Marton, 'ATAR Projekte 1945' *Klassiker der Luftfahrt*, 7/2015.
Szigeti, Marton, 'Hugo Harmens—vom Jungflieger zum Chefpiloten', *Klassiker der Luftfahrt*, 3/2013.
Szigeti, Marton, 'Ingenieur, Erfinder, Flugzeugbauer und Herausgeber Rhönvater Oskar Ursinus', *Klassiker der Luftfahrt*, 2/2016.
Supf, Peter, *Das Buch der deutschen Fluggeschichte* Zweiter Band, Drei Brunnen Verlag Stuttgart, 1958.
Wegerich, Hans, 'Das Doppelsitzer Segelflugzeug FES 530' Lehrmeister, *Deutsche Flugtechnik* 2/1960.

Endnotes:
SPECIALIST SELECTED DOCUMENTS AND MEDIA ARTICLES

1. Gründung der Gothaer Waggonfabrik vormals Fritz Bothmann & Glück Aktiengesellschaft am 30 July 1898, Handelsregister, Landesarchiv Thüringen—Staatsarchiv Gotha.
2. 'Das unsymmetrische Flugzeug – die Erfindung eines Schweizers', Schweizer Illustrierte Zeitung, 16 December 1942.
3. SVK Bericht 9 October 1916, Bundesarchiv, Militärarchiv Freiburg.
4. SVK Bericht 23 October 1916, Bundesarchiv, Militärarchiv Freiburg.
5. SVK Bericht 3 April 1917, Bundesarchiv, Militärarchiv Freiburg.
6. SVK-Bericht vom 17 May 1917, Bundesarchiv, Militärarchiv Freiburg.
7. SVK-Bericht 7 September 1917, Bundesarchiv, Militärarchiv Freiburg.
8. SVK Typenurteil 1515 (Gotha WD 20), Bundesarchiv, Militärarchiv Freiburg.
9. Brief Bayerische Waggon- und Flugzeugwerke an den Stadtrat Fürth, 17 July 1922.
10. Briefwechsel Kurt Toltz mit der Stadt Gotha vom 24 August 1926, Stadtarchiv Gotha.
11. Geschäftsbericht 1933 der Gothaer Waggonfabrik vom 17.10.1933, Stadtarchiv Gotha.
12. Bericht Dr. Schmidt, Oberbürgermeister der Stadt Gotha vom 17 October 1933, Stadtarchiv Gotha.
13. Schriftwechsel GWF-Stadt Gotha vom 15 December 1933, Stadtarchiv Gotha.
14. Deutsche Revisions- und Treuhandaktiengesellschaft Berlin, Jahresabschluss der Gothaer Waggonfabrik vom 31. Dezember 1942
Thüringisches Hauptstaatsarchiv Weimar, Waggonfabrik AG Gotha.
15. Einschreiben der GWF an den Reichsminister der Luftfahrt vom 5 May 1939 Thüringisches Hauptstaatsarchiv Weimar, Waggonfabrik AG Gotha.
16. Vortrag/Manuskript Dr August Kupper 'Der Entwurf eines schwanzlosen Versuchsflugzeuges Go 147', 19 March 1936.
17. Meldung der GWF über die Verschrottung des Flugzeugmusters Go 149 V-1, 1 November 1940 Thüringisches Hauptstaatsarchiv Weimar, Waggonfabrik AG Gotha
18. FAI Dokument Weltrekordflug der Go 150S vom 9 July 1939.
19. RLM-Amtschefbesprechung 37 vom 4 August 1942.
20. Lizenzvereinbarungen Heinkel He 45 und He 46 vom 11 December 1936
Thüringisches Hauptstaatsarchiv Weimar, Waggonfabrik AG Gotha .
21. Lieferstatistik der Gothaer Waggonfabrik vom 5 May 1938
Thüringisches Hauptstaatsarchiv Weimar, Waggonfabrik AG Gotha.
22. Lizenzvereinbarung Focke Wulf Fw 58 vom 30 June 1936.
Thüringisches Hauptstaatsarchiv Weimar, Waggonfabrik AG Gotha.
23. Lizenzvereinbarung Messerschmitt Bf 110 B vom 4 July 1938
Thüringisches Hauptstaatsarchiv Weimar, Waggonfabrik AG Gotha.

24 Verzeichnis der in 1942 gebuchten Rechnungen an das RLM
   Thüringisches Hauptstaatsarchiv Weimar, Waggonfabrik AG Gotha.
25 RLM Industrie-Lieferplan vom 31 January 1945.
26 Aktenvermerk über die Vorbesichtigung der Attrappe 8-229-V6 durch Oberleutnant Brüning vom 22.2.1945.
27 Bericht Auftriebsschlepp, Gothaer Waggonfabrik Aktiengesellschaft, Gotha, 12 October 1944.
28 Baubeschreibung Go P-60, Gothaer Waggonfabrik Aktiengesellschaft, Gotha, 28 January 1945.
29 Baubeschreibung Go P-60, Gothaer Waggonfabrik Aktiengesellschaft, Gotha, 11 March 1945.
30 Akte 9719, GWF 1941–1947, Stadtarchiv Gotha.
31 Beschluss der Thüringer Landesregierung vom18 July 1948 zur Überführung der Gothaer Waggonfabrik in Volkseigentum, Handelsregister
   Landesarchiv Thüringen—Staatsarchiv Gotha.
32 Schreiben vom Ministerium des Innern (Land Thüringen) am 7 May 1951 zur Löschung der Gotha-Ilmenauer Flugzeugbau G.m.b.H., Handelsregister
   Landesarchiv Thüringen—Staatsarchiv Gotha div. Wochenberichte des Seeflugzeug-Versuchskommandos Warnemünde 1915–1917 Bundesarchiv, Militärarchiv Freiburg SVK Atlas Seeflugzeuge Band 1/Band 2 1917/1918 Bundesarchiv, Militärarchiv Freiburg.